Bullshit Towers

Neoliberalism and managerialism in universities in Australia

Margaret Sims

PETER LANG

Oxford • Bern • Berlin • Bruxelles • New York • Wien

Bibliographic information published by Die Deutsche Nationalbibliothek.
Die Deutsche Nationalbibliothek lists this publication in the Deutsche National-
bibliografie; detailed bibliographic data is available on the Internet at
http://dnb.d-nb.de.

A catalogue record for this book is available from the British Library.

Cover image: Pamela Ann Murray
Cover design: Peter Lang.

ISBN 978-1-78997-812-4 (print) • ISBN 978-1-78997-809-4 (ePDF)
ISBN 978-1-78997-810-0 (ePub) • ISBN 978-1-78997-811-7 (mobi)

© Peter Lang AG 2020

Published by Peter Lang Ltd, International Academic Publishers,
52 St Giles, Oxford, OX1 3LU, United Kingdom
oxford@peterlang.com, www.peterlang.com

Margaret Sims hs asserted her right under the Copyright, Designs and Patents Act,
1988, to be identified as Author of this Work.

All rights reserved.
All parts of this publication are protected by copyright.
Any utilisation outside the strict limits of the copyright law, without
the permission of the publisher, is forbidden and liable to prosecution.
This applies in particular to reproductions, translations, microfilming,
and storage and processing in electronic retrieval systems.

This publication has been peer reviewed.

Printed in Germany

Contents

Figures

Foreword

I first met Margaret Sims when she was branch president of the National Tertiary Education Union (NTEU) at the University of New England and I was a member of the Council of the union's NSW Division. At the time she was under siege from New England's Chancellor, James Harris. Chancellor Harris, with the support of university management, had sought to ban Margaret, an elected member of university's Council for the preceding six years, from attending Council meetings on the grounds that she would be unable to act impartially because of her dual role as union Branch President and elected staff representative to Council. He wrote: 'Your conflict of interest will be present in relation to a wide range of issues, because a large number of matters considered by the council have a direct or indirect impact on staff, including NTEU members'.

In light of the fact that New England's two preceding chancellors had both faced inquiries into corruption, attempts by the university to limit transparency were deeply concerning.

The case was eventually settled and Margaret retained her place on Council, but the matter was important because it highlighted the connection between good governance, employee participation, and academic freedom. Academic freedom, a cornerstone of universities internationally and those in Australia in particular, is in part the principle that those who work at universities should be able to comment freely not only in the area of their specific academic interest but also on the operations of the universities at which they work. To seek to stifle transparency and critical inquiry into the function and operation of a university undermines not only good governance but also academic freedom.

Greater student, staff and union voice across our universities can shine a light on corrupt practices along the education supply chain as cases such as Gerd Schroeder-Turk's exposure of the difficulties international students face demonstrates. Employee engagement and voice can help hold universities to their mission as well as manage risk. Diversity of membership of a university council can act in the interests of a university as a whole even if individual members may oppose some actions of its current management. Employee voice may also act as a check on some managerialist practices such as those Margaret outlines.

Margaret's work as a union activist coupled with her scholarly approach have combined to produce a book that shines a much-needed light on the impacts of neoliberalism, cost cutting and managerialism on our universities. *Bullshit Towers* will probably offend some people, not least members of UNE's management. But those of us who labour at universities both here and overseas will recognise the management-imposed petty tyrannies that shape much of our working lives, the paltry restrictions that impede not only quality teaching and research but also impact negatively on the welfare of staff and students. Margaret's work illustrates the tensions between the rhetoric surrounding higher education in this country and the reality of ever-increasing workloads and employment insecurity.

For those who do not work in universities, *Bullshit Towers* brings to life the challenges neoliberalism has created for higher education in this country. The book is replete with unhappy (if entertaining) examples that illuminate management-driven absurdities. Like Raewyn Connell's recent The *Good University, Bullshit Towers* serves as a call to arms. It highlights why we need strong unions generally but across higher education in particular, and why we as a community need to organise to protect Australia's tertiary education sector. We do not have to accept higher education as shaped and defined by neoliberalist market forces. Indeed, we are obliged to oppose and counter its malign outcomes and ideology.

Dr Alison Barnes
National President
National Tertiary Education Union

CHAPTER I

Neoliberal managerial bullshit and its impact on education

I look at the document on my screen partly in horror and partly with a bit of an internal giggle. I totally get where Blair[1] is coming from, I really do. The report, written by her/his supervisor Sage, is so biased I wonder how Sage even had the gall to submit it to the Promotions Committee. I know when I read it on Friday I was utterly outraged. My instructions to Blair were to take time over the weekend in preparing the rebuttal. If necessary, I suggested s/he write an emotional response saying everything s/he wanted to say. Then delete that (metaphorically sending it up in flames) and prepare a factual rebuttal, with no emotion. What I am reading now has all the emotion removed but it is probably as far from factual (in terms of having evidence to support the claims) as it is possible to be. Blair has not only gone out on a limb here, s/he has fallen off the edge of the tree and maybe even over the edge of the world! I switch screens back to Blair's email intending to acknowledge receipt of the rebuttal and make a time to work on it. I re-read the email and freeze. Blair has actually sent this rebuttal to the Promotions Committee without waiting for my feedback. In horror I re-read the rebuttal and I identify several places where, if anyone other than myself were to read the document, it is possible that Blair could be targeted with a libel claim (or maybe it is slander – I can never remember which is which, but whatever it is legally, it's actionable). Whilst the material provided to the Promotions Committee is supposed to be confidential, I am certain that the material in the rebuttal would be used against Blair in particularly nasty ways, particularly given Sage's past history of making

---

[1]   I will use non-gender-specific English names for all those in my stories to ensure that gender and ethnicity cannot be used to identify people. For the same reason, and because I refuse to use the dehumanizing and disrespectful 'it' alternative, I will use the awkward s/he pronoun and his/her and her/his possessives.

Blair the target of multiple incidences of bullying (all defended using the argument of management prerogative despite clear evidence of unfair and unequal treatment). I seek urgent advice from my Industrial Officer Glenn and then call Blair. Glenn's advice, after reading the document, is that the rebuttal needs to be withdrawn urgently. With Blair's permission I contact HR asking that they withdraw the rebuttal so that the application stands without any rebuttal. They refuse. As far as they are concerned it is submitted and therefore must be attached to the application which will soon be circulated to the committee. In the end, the best option for Blair is to withdraw the entire promotion application. At the same time as I am working with Blair on this, I am aware that my colleague Sam is working with Chris, who also had a supervisor's report provided by Sage. Chris' supervisor's report also contains what we considered not only biased comments but downright lies. Sam and Chris work together on a rebuttal which is duly submitted. Some months later I am the NTEU observer on the Promotions Committee meeting that considers Chris' application and would have considered Blair's had it still been included. At this point in time, as the observer, I have access to all the documents (more recently NTEU observers have been refused access to the documents as it has been argued that the role is to observe and ensure fair process, not to have any input into content). I note the masterly rebuttal included in Chris' application and I wait the discussion on the application with interest because the rebuttal so clearly and logically demonstrates that the majority of the supervisor's report is incorrect. To my dismay I hear members of the committee making comments that suggest they take the supervisor's report as 100 per cent correct. At one point, following a comment made be a member about teaching performance (rated as terrible in the supervisor's report based on evidence that one of the units taught has such poor student evaluations that a unit action plan was warranted) I challenge the committee to verify their facts. The meeting is suspended whilst one member goes out to check the official database, and comes back in to confirm that Chris had not been responsible, nor had any involvement in the unit, at the time these student evaluations and the unit action plan were generated. Chris had been given the unit AFTER the unit action plan was required, as was clearly identified in the rebuttal. I argued that the committee were demonstratively unable to step aside from the bias generated in their thinking from the supervisor's report and that the fairest action would be to convene another group to examine Chris' application. I was told that of course the committee were able to act in an unbiased manner. I disagreed then (and said so, only to be ignored) and still do. Chris did not get promotion that year. Luckily with a change of supervisor the following year Chris was successful. At the end of the committee meeting the chair convened a discussion on the process, seeking suggestions as to concerns and improvements. I identified my concern with Sage's report noting the committee itself had investigated elements of it and found these to be untrue. I argued that producing a report with proven errors of fact was unprofessional, a clear indication of unfair bias on Sage's behalf, and there needed to be action taken. The response was, I considered, pathetically weak. Management would organise training for supervisors next year before supervisors wrote their reports. There was to be no consequence for Sage in having written a report that I considered biased, unfair, inaccurate and totally unprofessional. In fact, Sage remained supervising both Blair and Chris for quite some time until we were able to demonstrate a pattern of bias and unfair treatment (amounting to bullying) and successfully sought alternative supervisors for both members. Sage, however, remained in his/her management role.

I start with this story, not because it is dramatic or unusual but precisely the opposite: such events have happened far too frequently, generating in me a sense of outrage, and sometimes sheer disbelief, that people would behave this way. When did it become okay to lie about someone's work in a context that impacts on their career and on their professional identity? Why was it necessary to do this to someone else? When did the role of supervisor become one of knocking staff down rather than building them up? When did senior management lose the ability to address these behaviours, and appear to support them instead? Why does coming to work now make my stomach churn and my blood pressure skyrocket? Why has bullshit become the word I use most often when I read emails from management? And why does our building morning tea start feeling like a group therapy session?

I have worked in higher education for over 25 years with many years in the community-based sector beforehand. I have managed national programmes, large groups of staff, developed many degree programmes and lead/been through too many change management processes to even remember them all. I have been a Head of School and director of a Research Centre. I have been in a union all my working life, and as a manager, received the most amazing support from local union delegates. In these last years of my career I feel as if I am working in a different world; a world where I am disrespected, not trusted, and through speaking out, labelled a trouble-maker. I am not alone in feeling the changes that have occurred in the world of Australian higher education (Blackmore, 2015, p. 69; Connell, 2019a; Hil, 2012; Smyth, 2017; Watts, 2017; Withers, 2015). This is not a world in which I want to participate. How did things become like this? Is there a way to change so that I do not leave in despair but with a sense of hope that my younger colleagues can be as happy in their career as I once was?

In this book I will explore my sense-making of my working world. I believe that if I can understand what is going on, if I can pull together theories and hypotheses into a frame that makes sense to me, then I can perhaps not simply wallow in despair but identify what might be useful to drive change. In a sense I am researching myself, my experiences and my thoughts, filtered through my own understandings of the world and in-fluenced by as extensive a survey of the literature as I can manage without breaking my bank or blowing up my internet. To keep me focused, and to help me make absolutely certain that what I write is ethical (particularly in terms of anonymity for those about whom I write) I position this as research. I employ auto-ethnography as a tool to explore my experiences, to develop theory and to produce a model which helps me frame my ex-periences and my thinking. Because I position this as a piece of research, I will start with a literature review, proceed to discuss my methodology and then present several results chapters. Thus, to set the scene appropri-ately I need to explain what I mean when I use the term 'neoliberalism' and how I understand the literature positioning the impact of neoliberalism on the higher education sector. I need to explain what I understand as man-agerialism and how I believe the language of bullshit, used in neoliberal managerialism, communicates and shapes the world of higher education. Having clarified how I am using these concepts I will explain how I see them all fitting together and contributing to the world in which I am working. This then becomes the frame (conceptual model) I will use throughout the book to explore my experiences and to theorize from them.

Neoliberalism

I argue that neoliberalism, as I am using it in this book, is an ideology. Ideologies in general are not about what is true, but rather are ways of looking at, and interpreting the world, or in other words, making sense of the world. In the process of doing so, ideologies establish and legitimize particular elements and understandings as more powerful, more worthy than others (Klikauer & Tabassum, 2019; Robertson & Hill, 2014). In social psychology social representation theory captures this idea in the proposition that people chose (consciously or unconsciously) to belong to groups of others who share common understandings of the world, and that these common understandings shape their subsequent perceptions and understandings (Gjorgjioska & Tomicic, 2019) in a process something like a vicious cycle. However, ideologies, when they are lived by humans, morph and adapt to context; they are not absolutes (Fox & Alldred, 2017). Thus, the neoliberalism about which I write in this book is not a single hegemonic system but rather something that is evolving, full of contradictions and operating in different hybrid formations in different contexts (similar to the hybridisation discussed by Deckard & Shapiro, 2020; Kangas & Salmenniemi, 2016; Manathunga & Bottrell, 2019b; Stahl, 2019). It is rather like a many-headed beast that has created 'perverse and unintended outcomes' (O'Neill & Weller, 2013).

Arising in North America and Western Europe, neoliberalism has been adopted in many nations (Windle, 2019), including Australia, and imposed in many others through aid agencies and their development strategies (Bamberger, Morris, & Yemini, 2019). In areas of the world defined by Connell (2007, 2019a) as the global south, such impositions often result in a form of hybridisation where colonialism and White Privilege operate in conjunction with key drivers of neoliberal inequality. We may even be experiencing a mutation into some kind of post-neoliberal world (Lather, 2019; Means & Slater, 2019) where many of the principles of neoliberalism remain, but are modified to create a form of capitalism that operates without capital, where governance is mobile, intangible, and panoptic (Emma Rowe, 2019). This is a form of neoliberalism defined by 'deep marketisation' (Carroll & Jarvis, 2015) characterized by 'continuation of a modern day form of mal-development: economic growth that is inequitably captured, widening social stratification, reducing opportunities and mobility for lower socio-economic groups (especially those in agrarian settings), and a declining proportion of national wealth captured by wage labour' (p. 298).

What is clear is that neoliberalism can, and has been, applied to 'many a concept, place, thing, policy, process or space' (Emma Rowe, Lubienski, Skourdoumbis, Gerrard, & Hursh, 2019, p. 151). It can be seen as an 'economic theory, an ideology, a policy assemblage, a political discourse, and a mode of governance' (Blackmore, 2019a, p. 176), a form of social order (Cody, 2019), and 'the new common sense' (Carlen, 2018, p. 25). Further, Palumbo and Scott (2018, p. 4) position it as a 'toolkit of ideas, policies and instruments,' rather like a theory of everything (Rowlands & Rawolle, 2013). Neoliberalism has 'developed into a global political and cultural hegemony' (Bettache & Chiu, 2019, p. 11). It is important we do not allow this amorphous and non-specific approach to defining neoliberalism blunt our ability to think critically and thus risk 'perpetuating the dominant discourse ... rather than disrupting or challenging it' (Ertas & McKnight, 2019, p. 269). Thus, it is essential to spend some time sharing my understanding of neoliberalism as it is experienced in the context in which I live and work.

Anissimov (2013, p. 1) succinctly captures many of the key elements of neoliberalism as it is expressed politically; these being:

- People are not equal and never will be;
- 'Right is right. Left is wrong';
- Hierarchy is good; and
- Democracy is broken, cannot be fixed, and needs to be discarded.

An additional key element is the positioning of services and utilities as commodities rather than public goods (Carlen, 2018; Carroll, Clifton, & Jarvis, 2019). I'll work my way through these positions as I attempt to clarify what I mean when I use the term 'neoliberalism' in this book. To begin with, neoliberalism is often defined in economic terms. Using this focus, the market is considered as the most rational and sensible way of organizing society; what is good for organisations/corporations has to be good for society (Suleiman, 2019). Ultimately the role of government is to wind back state intervention (including state welfare) as it is assumed that markets will provide the necessary support (Lakes & Carter, 2011), creating 'market monsters' (Birch & Springer, 2019, p. 471). Underpinning the economic basis of neoliberalism is an assumption 'that collectively, human beings thrive under conditions of free competition, a meritocracy of wealth in which rewards go to each according to his ability' (Beattie, 2019, p. 89). As a consequence of this positioning, states around the world have increasingly imposed 'market-like disciplines and techniques' (Jayasuriya, 2015, p. 19) onto existing sectors (such as welfare, health, education) to create a form of regulatory state governance. In creating and maintaining this regulatory state, power has become more and more strongly vested in those who hold status and position so that 'existing neoliberalism serves to grant large corporations dominance over public life' (Beattie, 2019, p. 96). The assumption here is that when the elite are able to increase their wealth and power, they will use these to create opportunities for employment (and therefore access to wealth) for those less fortunate than themselves; a form of market organisation called trickle-down economics (Suleiman, 2019). This neoliberal focus positions inequality as desirable. Using this logic, society needs the elite as they, and not the state, will shape employment and access to wealth for those who are less fortunate.

The removal of state responsibility for citizen welfare marks a shift from public to private provision of services and a move away from the social state to a regulatory state whose key role is to create the contexts in which the elite can operate most effectively. Social democracy, positioning of the state as important in shaping economic and social interventions aimed at improving social equality, has over recent times become increasingly unpopular and many nations in the global north are moving away from a focus on social democratic ideas. In contrast, the political right places emphasis on the role of organisations and individuals rather than on the role of the state in shaping the way citizens live their lives. These movements reject 'big government', limit and/or reduce welfare provisions and often support big business through strategies such as reductions in tax.

They also result in 'renewed imperialism of law-and-order schemes on the global level (as in the endless "war on terror")' (Deckard & Shapiro, 2020, p. 2) which serve to clearly reify the elite and conversely, create a powerless class, those who are *not* of the elite. 'The exploitation of crises and disasters to force the imposition of austerity and structural adjustment' (Deckard & Shapiro, 2020, p. 2) which press more heavily on the powerlesss than on the elite and 'the increased biopolitical control of individuals by the state' (ibid., p. 2) result in a perception that workers (as distinct from managers, CEOs, etc.) are positioned as inferior, needing to be managed and organised and in need of guidance in order to function most effectively in producing wealth for the elite. I am reminded of the wonderful quote from George Orwell's *Animal Farm* (Orwell, 1944; ebook 2016, no page numbers): 'No one believes more firmly than Comrade Napoleon that all animals are equal. He would be only too happy to let you make your decisions for yourselves. But sometimes you might make the wrong decisions, comrades, and then where should we be?'

Workers are shaped into becoming neoliberal citizens, who dutifully spend their working hours producing for their employer, and increasingly spend their leisure hours using their hard-earned income to consume products corporations have persuaded them they need in order to live the good life. Giroux (2015, p. 6) argues people are seduced 'into chasing commodities, and infantilized ... through the mass production of easily digestible entertainment, disposable goods, and new scientific advances in which any viable sense of agency was undermined.' The neoliberal state, and its accompanying hegemonic ideology, create a context where all that we are as individuals (our values, beliefs and identities) is commodified, and judged against material standards. Consumerism, and pursuit of material goods diverts attention from social injustices and the critical thought necessary for democratic decision-making so that the elite are free to 'do as they please' (Chomsky, 2016, p. 56). Participation in democratic debate and critical thinking are no longer valued, and less and less often practised. We see increasingly that popularity and power are based on the ability to spin a good story, rather than on any resemblance to truth (the lack of concern for the truth evident in Trump's campaign and his supporters is a case in point (Ball, 2017)). Dissent is perceived as traitorous, and as such, a legitimate target for punitive action (Foroughi, Gabriel, & Fotaki, 2019). This is evident despite changes in Australian legislation designed to protect whistle-blowers (from July 2019 changes to the Corporations Act 2001 – see <https://asic.gov.au/about-asic/asic-investigations-and-enforcement/whistleblowing/>). For example, the whistle-blower in a recent case involving the Australian Tax Office was sacked, faces 66 charges and possibly over 160 years in prison (Khadem, 2019a). For many, actions such as this represent a significant shift away from democracy (Klikauer & Tabassum, 2019) and a shift towards various forms of state authoritarianism (Means & Slater, 2019), represented by the term authoritarian-neoliberal state (Juego, 2018).

Along with this reification of inequality and inequitable access to wealth and power, comes the neoliberal positioning of individuals as responsible for themselves. Individuals are positioned as rational beings capable of making choices, and therefore must accept the consequences of their choices. These choices are thought to be equally available to all, irrespective of gender, race, socioeconomic positioning and age (Blackmore, 2019a). All people are thought to have equal opportunity, and, because of this, they are expected to have equal ability to succeed. This is accompanied by a perception that we are all responsible for what we consume. Under neoliberalism utilities such as water and electricity, and services such as education, are commonly privatized, because individuals are expected to purchase these in the same way as they purchase consumer goods. Use of these utilities and services is thought to lead to private good and therefore, it is expected that private individuals should pay for what they use.

Given the market focus of neoliberalism, individuals are valued for what they contribute to the market thus success is equated to money and people begin to be perceived less as people, and more as human capital that can be exploited for labour and whose need for employment can be used as a mechanism of control (Bourassa, 2019). Those who do not earn wealth (and who are therefore not successful) are positioned as failures; in other words, individuals are expected to succeed in the labour market with minimal or no state protection. Work that does not generate income or is not associated with money (for example care: Askins & Blazek, 2017) is not valued. Work itself has become so important that many people spend their lives doing work they do not enjoy, believing that their work contributes little or nothing of value to the world in which they live, yet they persevere because to fail to do so would position them as losers and of no value at all (Graeber, 2019). They continue to operate in this manner not only because of the power of the elite to prescribe how they live their lives, but because they have learned to value employment and income over quality of life. Many years ago Freire (1973) identified this ability of those in power to shape the perceptions of people who are oppressed so that oppression becomes self-sustaining. Success and failure are not only defined by the powerful, but are accepted as the standards against which lives should be lived by those who are oppressed. Individuals manage their lives according to the rules they perceive as universal and this deception is self-sustaining (Davis, 2017) and accepted uncritically. At least 15 years ago (Taylor, 2003, p. 16) warned that the outcome of this positioning put nations at risk of losing their ability to achieve 'important strategic targets with an amnesiac's sense of timing and the marksmanship of Mr Magoo' because they will simply not have the human capital available with the ability to think beyond the boundaries of the narrow boxes into which they have been educated to place themselves.

It is important for the powerful to control their human capital so accompanying neoliberalism is an increase in surveillance and accountability through audit regimes. Emma Rowe (2019, p. 276) talks about 'digitised panopticism' made possible through ongoing improvements in information technology, so that it is no longer uncommon for employers to use electronic means of surveillance (for example recording all phone calls), and to peruse employees' social media activity. Employees are increasingly limited in their social media activity as many employers do not allow any criticism of the organisation or its managers to be posted online, and controversial views posted on social media may led to formal disciplinary proceedings (Hayes, 2019). This is linked to the concept of academic freedom; the ability to speak critically in the public and professional domains. Orr (2019) argues we face increasing threats to this, many of them indirect but just as powerful in limiting informed critique as are more direct threats. These increasing restrictions force workers into complying, although for many, compliance may be tokenistic (Connell, 2019a). However, requirements to demonstrate compliance often mean that workers spend more time doing this accountability work than actually doing the work for which they are employed (Spicer, 2018), a diversion of labour that often results in undermining the purpose of the organisation, making the organisation less, rather than more efficient (Graeber, 2019).

Neoliberalism in education

Higher education (and education generally) in Australia, along with the UK and New Zealand operates in a context strongly influenced by neoliberalism (Rodgers Gibson, 2019; Shore & Wright, 2019; Thornton, 2015). Neoliberalism 'is an ideology that saturates the educational land-scape, shaping every educational practice in its image' (Reid, 2019, pp. 153–154). The assumption underpinning this is that the ideas and processes that shape the way corporations/businesses operate should also shape the way universities and other educational institutions run. A business-like approach is seen as the way to improve the sector, enhance quality and ensure that public funding is spent in the most efficient manner possible (Lakes & Carter, 2011). Higher education is thought to operate in a market, just as does any other business resulting in the 'subordination of academic activity to commercial goals' (Taberner, 2018, p. 130).

There is considerable debate in the literature as to the relevance of the market concept as it applies to higher education. Universities are positioned by government (and, in Australia, have universally accepted this role) as separate organisations who are competing in the market for students (Connell, 2019a). The 'product' marketed by universities is identified as a qualification which is sold to students in order for them to gain employment (Hil, 2012). It is even possible to go so far as to call universities shopping malls from where students purchase job qualifications (Edgar & Edgar, 2019). Alternatively, the product offered by universities is sometimes argued to be the human capital needed by individuals seeking status, advantaging them in competition for employment in competitive markets (Bamberger et al., 2019). This position makes the assumption that education cannot be bought but status can. Taking a slightly different perspective Watts (2017) suggests that rather than purchasing employment for the sake of status, students are purchasing employment in order to earn sufficient income to buy material goods that will serve to identify their status in the world.

Irrespective of the product sold by universities (a qualification, status or the ability to pursue material goods), as consumers, students are expected to act as passive recipients of what universities sell them (Connell, 2019a); they are expected to consume the product offered to them. Uncertainty around the nature of the product they are purchasing (Watts, 2017) often results in a disjunction between what students think they are purchasing, what universities think they are selling, and what academic staff actually deliver. It is worth noting here that a recent survey demonstrated students believe that universities should not only provide them with a qualification, universities should also provide them with a job on graduation (J. Ross, 2019e). The link between purchasing a qualification and the employment this leads to, is internalised by most students and thus shapes their expectations of the product they are purchasing. In Australia, this link was reinforced by the federal government with the Minister of Education recently announcing a large proportion of funding for universities linked to graduate employment rates (Havergal, 2019). The reality of increased fees for students reinforces their perception that they are attending university in order to purchase a product (Connell, 2019a).

Supporting the positioning of students as purchasers of a product comes the marketing needed to sell that product to the student market. Universities have significantly increased their marketing budgets over the past decade (Hil, 2012) and are particularly concerned to manage image/brand. Watts (2017) reports, for example, that the University of New England increased its marketing budget by 77 per cent between the years 2009 and 2013. Over that same time period, enrolments increased by about 18 per cent.

Given a significant element of marketing is based on consumer evaluations, there is an expectation that students will be supplied with what they want in order to return the favour by evaluating their university experiences positively. Although the research indicates students are not always clear on what they want (Watts, 2017), there is a general consensus that students are increasingly expecting an relatively easy passage through their studies, where difficult or challenging material is no longer offered to them because of fears that this will trigger poor evaluations and impact on market position. For example in America, concerns are expressed that any material that might trigger an emotional response from any student in a class needs to be accompanied by a trigger warning so as not to risk challenging students' values and beliefs (American Association of University Professors, 2014; Furedi, 2017). As a consequence Watts (2017) and Furedi (2017) argue that curriculum is simplified so that students obtain good grades and respond with high customer satisfaction ratings. This leads to poorer student learning, fewer intellectual challenges and pressures on academics to pass students. Hill (2004, p. 504) positions this has as the 'compression and repression of critical space in education today.' Such a lack of focus on student critical thinking ultimately results in the integrity of qualifications being compromised, in an era when quality is highly scrutinized.

Accompanying the positioning of students as passive consumers is the positioning of academics as the human capital needed to deliver the product. In the business world, successful product is standardised, so customers are guaranteed to all receive the same quality product for their money. As the human capital delivering this product in the higher education sector, academics are coming under increasing pressure to standardise their teaching. Given the intangible interactions between teachers and students cannot be measured and therefore are impossible to standardise, what becomes identified as the product sold is the actual concrete teaching materials. Thus, a lecture becomes a verbal set of materials transmitted to students (its equivalent being a written paper), often prepared well before it is actually delivered. Good-quality teaching thus becomes more closely linked with the traditional lecture system simply because it is the most efficient way to standardise the product delivered to students (Watts, 2017). Financial pressures also support this model of teaching, given one academic can deliver a lecture to a large number of students. Standardisation of teaching is accompanied by standardisation of assessment (Raaper, 2019) so that all students are required to deliver the same work marked to the same standards. Given increasing student:staff ratios and growing workload, assessments move more and more towards computer-marked activities such as quizzes rather than essays and reports where a reasoned argument is required (Manathunga & Bottrell, 2019a). Thus the product increasingly delivered to students is not based on what the research identifies as high-quality teaching and learning, but rather follows an information transmission model 'augmented by the hollow promise of on-line "delivery" of learning resources' (Watts, 2017, p. 226).

Managerialism

The ways in which neoliberalism impacts on culture, individual psychology and our economic and political systems creates a zeitgeist (Eagleton-Pierce, 2019; Samier, 2018) which has bred a way of managing organisations I am calling managerialism. In a sense neoliberalism can be thought of as the macro-level ideology which, when enacted at the micro-level within organisations, manifests as managerialism. In the literature, when this is enacted within public service organisations it often referred to as new public management (NPM: Watts, 2017). I will subsume NPM into the term managerialism in this book to avoid the debate as to whether universities can be defined as public service organisations or not.

Managerialism, like neoliberalism, can be defined in different ways thus it is necessary to identify what I mean when I use the term. First, managerialism is not the same as management. Taylor (2003, p. 5) argues that management is the 'necessary organising activities required in any large, complex organisation' whereas managerialism is 'the petty self-perpetuating creation of needless bureaucracy and anti-professional controls that are rife' in large, complex organisations. Managerialism is positioned as a neutral activity to the extent that it is argued that it is better for managers not to have an extensive understanding of the sector in which they are operating as managers (Blackmore, 2019a). In other words, being a good manager is thought to depend on a range of skills and knowledges that are independent of the sector in which they are being applied, and therefore are generalisable across all different contexts. Managerialism is based on the assumption that better management will result in better solutions for all our social problems and will make organisations maximally effective and efficient. Organisations are structured along hierarchical lines (Taberner, 2018) and this hierarchical nature led Klikauer and Tabassum (2019) to position managerialism as a return to feudalism. In a rather tongue in cheek fashion, they claim: 'Managerialism mixes Orwellian-style "some animals are more equal than others" with Big Brother style workplace surveillance' (p. 90). In discussing this point, Morrish (2016, p. 1) argues the purpose of managerialism is to render 'employees subordinate.'

In enacting neoliberalism through managerialism in universities, the fundamental nature of academia is changed (Taberner, 2018). Democratic decision-making and a focus on public service is lost (Blackmore, 2019a; Connell, 2019a) and staff are expected to be compliant and docile rather than agentic (Manathunga & Bottrell, 2019b). Academics are no longer accountable to the public but rather to their supervisors and more power is placed in the hands of management and external consultants (Blackmore, 2019a). Whilst it is easy to claim that these changes arise from external pressures (macro-level neoliberal ideology which creates the context in which organisations must operate), there is also evidence that university managements have accepted such modes of operation, and thus universities have, in fact, become 'corporatized from within' (Connell, 2019a, p. 119). As such, the hierarchies that privilege those with power become self-perpetuating as those in such positions have no motivation to change systems, and those oppressed by the systems struggle to find agency and power to challenge persistent inequities.

Accountability has become a tool used by management to ensure staff perform in ways that produce the standardised, measurable product they believe the organisation delivers. In higher education, given that good-quality teaching can be neither measured nor standardised, this means that accountability regimes measure other elements of academic work. There is growing concern that adherence to such regimes significantly decreases the available time to do the actual work for which people are employed to produce (Klikauer & Tabassum, 2019). It can feel as if the real work has somehow to be fitted around this compliance work (Spicer, 2018). Filling

in forms and other administrative, compliance tasks rarely improve organisational performance, but serve to justify managerialism (Klikauer &
Tabassum, 2019). Along with this comes the proliferation of management
and supervisory positions needed to monitor compliance, a phenomena
(Watts, 2017, p. 182) calls 'administrative bloat.' Requirements to conform
and perform imposed on workers rarely generate rewards (apart from the
salary received) whereas it is not uncommon for the kudos for improvements in organisational performance to be claimed by management and
attributed to management supervision structures and processes rather
than recognised as the outcome of the work performed by staff (Klikauer
& Tabassum, 2019).

Bullshit

Macro-level neoliberalism enacted in organisations at the micro-level
through managerialism uses language to name, and therefore shape, perceptions of reality. The language we use to talk about our experiences actually frames our understandings (Watts, 2017) which we then share with
others and in turn, influence their understandings (Contandriopoulos,
2019). Thus language is an essential element of culture (Gaztambide-
Fernández, 2011). In the culture (or zeitgeist) of organisations, the language used both reflects, and shapes, neoliberalism and managerialism. In
naming the world within managerial organisations, language is required
to justify the neoliberal requirements of hierarchies, standardisation,
accountability regimes, lack of trust in workers and disregard for social
justice. This language was labelled bullshit over 10 years ago (Frankfurt,
2005) and since that time there have been numerous researchers who have
engaged with the concept of bullshit language and its role in reinforcing
neoliberal managerialism (Ball, 2017; Christensen, Kärreman, & Rasche,
2019; Davis, 2017; Graeber, 2019, to name a few).

This extensive scholarship makes it necessary to clearly identify what
I mean when I use the terms bullshit/bullshit language. In his original

essay Frankfurt (2005) argued that bullshit was phony; language designed to deliberately hide the fact that the speaker does not understand what s/he is saying. People, he argues, do this when they want to convey that they belong to a privileged group. Since that time, a number of authors have attempted to examine what is meant by the concept of phony or bullshit language. Spicer (2018, p. 53) for example, argues that bullshit language is 'something with a meaning which is unclear ... cannot be made into clear statements that we understand, without changing the meaning of what is said.' Bullshit is 'obscure, empty or pretentious talk' that has become the new norm (Christensen et al., 2019, p. 2). This language often sounds profound but its weighty sounding words hide a complete lack of clarity and meaning. Bullshit has 'no practical conceptual value' (Contandriopoulos, 2019, p. 1). Going further than most, Ball (2017, p. 5) argues that bullshit is 'a catch-all word to cover mis-representation, half-truths and outrageous lies alike.' Bullshit can even function to obscure hypocrisy so that one thing can be said but something completely different enacted. For example (J. Ross, 2019c, p. 2), commenting on a recent Review of Provider Category Standards in higher education in Australia claims the review document demonstrates: 'the most fervent opponents of the creation of teaching-only universities in Australia are the most enthusiastic recruiters of teaching-only academics.'

Bullshit language is used as a signal of belonging, created by the elite to identify their group (Klikauer & Tabassum, 2019). For example, jargon creates a boundary between those 'in the know' and outsiders, functioning rather like 'a linguistic barbed wire fence' (Spicer, 2018, p. 11). This was demonstrated in the study of students attending elite private schools undertaken by Gaztambide-Fernández (2011). He reported that the key benefit the students saw themselves gaining was the language they needed to signal to others their membership of the elite, and to signal to themselves that they deserved their placement in the elite. Thus bullshit language is a signalling behaviour, designed to maintain group membership and thus individual comfort, belonging and psychological wellbeing (Spicer, 2018). Bullshit language tells listeners a lot about the person: who that person is and who that person wants to be (Davis, 2017).

Having gained competency in the language that signals one belongs to the elite, there is little desire to critique either the language or the concepts (or lack of concepts) it is used to convey. Rather, to maintain group belonging there is an expectation that one does not critique, as to do so is likely to jeopardize group membership (Ball, 2017). As a consequence, group membership is maintained by choosing not to think about issues deeply, a form of laziness where we internalise behaviour modelled by others in the group without thinking about what that behaviour conveys to others, nor about its morality (Davis, 2017). Thus, use of bullshit may signal a complete lack of understanding of concepts, or simply the lack of ability to describe what is meant (Christensen et al., 2019). Membership in the elite is maintained by choosing not to investigate ideas deeply but to simply pass on the lack of clarity to those further down in the hierarchy, whilst trying to sound profound when doing so.

Creating this link between bullshit language and belonging to the elite means that workers who are not currently members of the elite focus on learning the right language with the goal of improving their status and ultimately joining the desired group. In order to do so they learn not to question the language, but rather how to use it most effectively to demonstrate their leadership potential. As a consequence they become 'unwitting conduits for ideas, which are unclarifiable and unsuggestive' (Spicer, 2018, p. 54), spreading not only the bullshit language, but the meaningless ideas upon which it is based. This can often be without a conscious attempt to deceive, but the communication of surface ideas where there has been little or no critical analysis reinforces the role of empty words and phrases as forming the gateway for progress into the elite. Thus it can appear as if promotion hinges not on hard work, but on some kind of magical transformation that results from using the right bullshit, at the right time, to the right people. As Bottrell and Keating (2019, p. 170) explain:

> Just as non-compliant staff are declared redundant, re-located away from peer networks or starved of support for career progression, the 'resilient' and 'flexible' staff are promoted and rewarded for their capacity to adapt to change.

Because bullshit language is unclear and usually meaningless, a gap is created between those in the elite who speak bullshit, and the workers who have to actually put these meaningless ideas into action (Spicer, 2018). When things do not work as planned, it is then easy for the elite to blame the workers. The elite (managers) are 'drawn together in a web of denial which frees members from the inconvenient truth or "troubling recognition" of wrongdoing while the more powerful get to "shrug off the responsibility" for the harmful effects of their action, thereby ensuring legitimacy for further wrongdoing' (Bessant, 2015, p. 255). Shrugging off responsibility is justified by those in the elite who have simply followed the rules as they saw them (Apple, 2017), and given they have followed the rules, the workers must be to blame when things do not work as expected.

The characterizations of bullshit as 'mis-representations, half-truths' (Ball, 2017, p. 5) and as language that is 'obscure, empty or pretentious' (Christensen et al., 2019, p. 2) are positions I am comfortable accepting, however I question the portrayal of bullshit as 'outrageous lies' (Ball, 2017, p. 5). I do not in the least doubt that there are times when bullshit segues into lies, but I do not think that falsehoods are necessarily deliberate (though they can be at times). The intent to deceive is, I believe, not always present when bullshit language is used. Rather it's use is, as discussed above, to act as a shield to hide one's lack of understanding, one's desire to belong and therefore one's unwillingness to challenge the norms of the elite group.

Bullshit language, used in the higher education sector, is not only used by managers to create boundaries around themselves as the managerial elite, but also to position the education sector as legitimately part of the business world, so that what is perceived as business-like approaches (such as neoliberal managerialism) are legitimised (Davis, 2017). Thus bullshit language, enacted in the neoliberal, managerial higher education sector is (Klikauer & Tabassum, 2019, p. 98):

designed to support what ideology sets out to achieve, namely three things:

- to camouflage contradictions (e.g. the fact that workers and management have different interests on wages, working time and general working conditions),
- to cement domination (e.g. managerial domination over workers), and finally
- to prevent emancipation (e.g. by obscuring the true affairs of work through, for example, putting up a smokescreen called business bullshit).

It is possible to argue that the language of bullshit break the links between language and action (Alvesson & Spicer, 2016; Spicer, 2018), language and thinking (Klikauer, 2013; Klikauer & Tabassum, 2019) and language and reality (Contandriopoulos, 2019). Bullshit speaks a culture into reality where action, thinking and reality are not the desired outcomes of the spoken word. It is possible then to argue that bullshit language makes a post-truth world possible; a world where empty words are normalized (Foroughi et al., 2019) and where truth matters less than populist appeal to emotions (Ball, 2017). In the end what matters is the interpretation or spin given to the narrative, not the truth underpinning it (Davis, 2017).

Summary

In this chapter I have introduced the three main threads through which I will examine my experiences in higher education. Whilst I will demonstrate how I tie these threads together in the following chapter, it is useful at this point to summarize they key elements of each of these threads as I am using them in this book. Neoliberalism reifies a divide between the elite and the workers; this gap is desirable, as it is through state support for the elite that opportunities are then trickled down to the workers. Neoliberalism involves the imposition of marketization onto the higher education sector. I argue education itself cannot be sold. Instead, as customers, students are buying both a qualification and the status a qualification brings in terms of employment and future income. Such outcomes enable graduates to position themselves as good neoliberal citizens who support the neoliberal state by increasing their purchasing power. Thus neoliberalism as an ideology situates ideal students as compliant, willing to consume unquestionably the information provided in their studies. Knowledge itself is only valued in terms of its contribution to employment related skills. Teaching becomes the transmission of employment-required knowledge, often constrained by external accreditation bodies whose standards are set by employers. The process of teaching is not valued because it is not measurable; what is valued is that which is quantifiable (such as student satisfaction scales, test results and measures of retention). The need to measure to provide evidence of accountability creates a divide between those delivering the teaching and those responsible for measuring and determining the worth of what is done.

Neoliberalism is enacted in organisations through managerialism; behaviours that act to reify standardisation, accountability and inequality, the touchstones of neoliberalism. Managerialism is based on hierarchies with those actually delivering the product to market (i.e. the teaching) located at the lower ends of the hierarchy. Associated with this subordinate positioning is the assumption that workers cannot be trusted and therefore need to be extensively supervised to ensure their work is done appropriately. In higher education this becomes visible through managerial imposition of standards and accountability mechanisms that feel overly onerous to the recipients, to the extent that there is major concern that so much time is spent performing these administrative tasks that the real work of academics can only be done in private time outside of work hours. Given quality is identified as what can be (and is) measured, there are concerns that the intangible work that many believe better represents good quality is becoming more and more difficult to perform.

Tying the ideology of neoliberalism with its micro-level organisational enactment through managerialism is the language of bullshit. Language is powerful and shapes culture. The language of bullshit uses the concepts of neoliberalism and names them in the managerial culture of higher education. Through naming, bullshit language creates a culture that becomes self-reinforcing. Bullshit language communicates the interpretation or spin used to reflect the values and practices of neoliberal managerialism and functions to obscure any truth that might underlie the organisational world. One needs to speak the language of bullshit to be identified by managers as a potential leader. Once in the management group, the language of bullshit must be spoken to maintain one's position. Given bullshit language is unclear, and hides a lack of coherence, substance and reality, the divide between those who speak the language and those who are meant to implement what it actually does not say, grows ever wider. The language of bullshit speaks the neoliberal managerial culture into reality and thus shapes the experiences of those living and working in that culture. Bullshit language creates a post-truth organisational world.

CHAPTER 2

The research process

I see that I have an email from the Ethics Committee and make a mental note to open it later when I feel I have the head space to deal with what will undoubtedly (from many previous experiences) be some kind of bullshit. I head off down to morning tea and an interesting and laughter-filled interaction with my colleagues, necessary for my sanity. Later in the day, sitting in my home office, I finally screw up the fortitude to open the email. My home office is one of my favourite rooms in the house. It has a wall of bookshelves containing much of my leisure reading, and a large glass door that opens onto the deck and the back yard so that I feel some degree of connection with the trees and plants that nearly fill the space between the deck and the back fence. My office reminds me that I have a life outside work, but it also reminds me that I have a work identity and credibility built up over many years. I feel safe in this space. The email I turn to relates to a research project for which I have completed data collection and am now writing up in a series of journal articles. Much of this writing has (and continues) to happen sitting at this very desk. It's much easier to find the focused time to write in my home office rather than my work office. The data is stored on the cloud as required and I have recently downloaded a selection of interview transcripts that I am using for the most recent article I am writing. Working with these transcripts directly off the cloud is problematic (not the least a costly impost on my home wireless) so it's easier for me to download the transcripts I have chosen at work and store them on my laptop for easy access. Last month I had been required to write a final report for the Ethics Committee given that data collection had been completed. In this final report I had been honest and identified that whilst all the data was stored on the cloud as was required by university policy, I had a small selection currently duplicated on my laptop in order to perform the necessary analyses for my paper. I identified in the report that once this work was completed, I would delete these files off my laptop as per policy. I open the email and read it. I am told that my final report is not acceptable because I did not state in it where my laptop was located. I sigh, roll my eyes, and walk into the kitchen to make myself a coffee. Like most staff, the main reason I work on a laptop rather than a desktop is that I can take it with me wherever I work – usually this is at the office at work and in my home office but I also travel (for example, six weekly meetings in Sydney) and take my laptop with me when I do so that I can work wherever I am. I rather thought that was the whole purpose of a laptop so find the requirement to identify WHERE my laptop is, is ridiculous, particularly given that I have identified in the report that the laptop is password protected as is standard. With tongue somewhat in cheek I send an email to the contact person for the ethics committee that says the location of my laptop is with me. The following day I get a reply: I must paste this exact response in the final report and resubmit the final report. At this point I feel really aggrieved: my meaningless and obvious (I call the Homer Simpson 'duh' to mind) reply appears acceptable – where else would my laptop be but with me? I decline to waste my time pasting this phrase into the final report – it is so obvious that I do not believe it should be necessary to do so nor do I want to spend time figuring out where in the report it is supposed to go. I am informed, again by email, that this means my final report is now outstanding and will be identified as such until such time as I resubmit the report with this amendment. I still have not done so. I am identified as non-compliant by the committee. I'm not sure if my paranoia reads into the response a somewhat hidden threat that this non-compliance will impact on future ethics applications. As I have not made any (nor do I intend to do so), I can't tell.

Research has different meanings to different people and can be performed in many different ways. I began my academic career studying psychology, archaeology and physical anthropology. In my psychology papers (units were called papers in my undergraduate degree) I was required to study positivism and to pass a paper on statistics. This way of looking at the world was positioned as the only way to undertake research and I had no idea that there were other ontologies and epistemologies. My anthropology studies were in physical anthropology rather than social or cultural anthropology and positivism was also the main research approach there. It was not until I began teaching at university much later that I learned about other ways of looking at, and researching in, the world.

I remember the first student I supervised who was doing post graduate research using an interpretivist framework. We had an uphill battle to get the research accepted by the university for which I was then working. The research was considered second class because it did not involve randomised control trials. Instead, the student undertook over 80 individual, semi-structured interviews, a workload that these days I would absolutely refuse to countenance. At the time this was considered necessary by the student and the supervision team in order to be considered minimally acceptable by the university research hierarchy. The idea of researching oneself, of examining one's own experiences, would have been considered anathema, and to be honest, I would then have had some sympathy for that position myself. Luckily, with time and experience I learned to see the world differently, and learned to understand the value of a range of different approaches I would never have considered in my earlier years as an academic. I began to feel really comfortable in the world of interpretivism. Over the years as I was introduced to critical research and post-colonial research I expanded my horizons and began to use a range of different approaches in my work and in recent years I have begun to think about new materialism and post humanism.

This book is based on an approach to research called autoethnography. There are a number of reasons why I have chosen this approach. The fundamental reason is that I want to ensure that what I write is ethical. Inevitably other people are involved in the reflections I present of my experiences. Some of these people are peers, some are people I have supported when doing case work for the National Tertiary Education Union (NTEU), the union covering university employees in Australia (both academic and professional staff), and some are managers. I cannot offer useful reflections without including other people however their anonymity must be preserved at all times. Given I am used to operating within a research framework, I thought that the best way to do this is to treat this work as a research project. The ethical constraints that govern research should therefore be accessible to me in this work, and I will use these principles to continually scrutinize my work to ensure compliance.

In framing this chapter, I will therefore use the standard structure of a research proposal. That means I will begin with a discussion of ontology/

epistemology and conceptual framework. This latter is necessary as it takes the material from the previous chapter and demonstrates how I see these factors interacting. The model I develop to show this then frames the structure of the remainder of this book. This will be followed by a discussion on methodology and method – in this case autoethnography. I will identify the context in which my reflections – the data for the study – are generated and the process by which I have developed and analysed the reflections. I will provide a further discussion on ethics as they relate to this study and an outline of the structure of the remaining chapters of the book.

Epistemology and Ontology

In an interpretivist ontology there is no single reality or single truth (N. Wright & Losekoot, 2016). Social constructivism, as a form of interpretivism, places humans in the position of constructing their own realities so that there are as many different realities or truths as there are humans engaged in the research context (Keaton & Bodie, 2011; Khalifa, 2010; Pilgrim, 2017). New materialism and post humanism take this ontological positioning further by de-centring humans and arguing that rather than humans acting on material objects and thus shaping their world, instead humans and material objects both influence each other, and it is the interaction of these that combine to shape the world (Feely, 2019; Fox & Alldred, 2017, 2018; Jagger, 2015). Here, a reality is supposed to exist based on material objects, and adding to this reality is the reality humans construct through their beliefs, values and behaviours. I am drawn to the concept of de-centring humans and giving equal status to the idea that material objects also contribute in significant ways to shaping the world and our actions in the world, however I am reluctant to claim that this study is located squarely in this ontology. Rather, I prefer to take a somewhat eclectic position and claim that, in the process of reflecting on my own reality, I will seek to reflect on the way I perceive material elements of that world impacting on me. Given this is hardly a de-centring of the human, this work cannot be located in either new materialism or post humanism but rather in a traditional social constructivist ontology, with attempts to reach out and create a more defractive assemblage of data than might traditionally be expected. My approach is rather like the lyrics in the song written by Paul Anka, and recorded by Frank Sinatra in 1969: 'I did it my way.'

Given this ontological position, the related epistemology places interpretation of reality as the key epistemological task (Jakubik, 2011; Tuli, 2010). Meaning or understanding are, in effect, my property, given meaning is expected to arise from my own reflections of my own experiences. This epistemological position requires an assumption that there is some underlying meaning that can be extracted from the data, and this underlying meaning, once understood, will enable me and my readers to better understand their experiences, their reality. Along with better understanding might then come the ability to change things in the world. This idea of change is the underpinning concept in critical research (Denzin, 2017; Tyson, 2006). Freire used this concept in his work, and in particular the concept that the powerful are able to impose their own understandings of the world upon those who are oppressed, who come to internalise these understandings and accept their position as inferior (Freire, 1973). Gaining an understanding of this transfer process of the world view from the powerful onto the oppressed then enables those who are oppressed to reframe their understandings of the world and thus challenge their oppression. This idea flows through into a range of different critical theory-based approaches including post-colonialism (K. Martin, 2018; Sims & Tiko, 2019), critical race theory (Ledesma & Calderón, 2015; Montoya & Sarcedo, 2018), white privileging (Radd & Grosland, 2018) and southern theory (Connell, 2007; Takayama, Heimans, Amazan, & Maniam, 2016) to name but a few. Deleuzian thinking (Deleuze, 1995; Deleuze & Guattari, 1987) positions this as a need to challenge everything, every assumption, every belief, everything that is taken for granted, every experience in order to identify the logic imposed through the operation of the dominant discourse, to free oneself from that discourse and think differently. In this study I argue that understanding my experiences in higher education creates an opportunity to articulate the oppressive strategies being used by those in power to place me in an inferior position. Having done so, I argue I am better able to determine effective strategies to resist this positioning, and better able to offer suggestions to others operating in similar contexts. Ultimately, I believe, more effective strategies of resistance have the potential to challenge the ideology I believe is driving the behaviour of those in power, although I acknowledge the difficulty in doing so, as those who have the most to benefit from the current system are those who have the least desire to change.

Conceptual framing

The conceptual framing of this study is outlined in Figure 1. I argue the broader ideology of neoliberalism creates a zeitgeist in political, economic and social contexts that reifies certain values that in turn are translated into behaviour within organisations through managerialism. In this sense I am using neoliberalism in a manner that Deckard and Shapiro (2020, p. 15) prefer to identify as neoliberalisation; that is, ongoing and evolving:

> material processes and technologies of capitalist penetration and development ... forms of neoliberal thought that occupy the cultural dominant but are nonetheless striated by internal conflicts and inter-capitalist competition and unevenly implemented across the world-system, as well as the broader cultural forms through which the neoliberal world-system is constituted and represented as a lived reality.

Neoliberalism, as an ideology, impacts through a slow, continual drip (rather like that of the ancient Chinese torture) of patterns of interactions, habits, memories and experiences (Fox & Alldred, 2017) that combine to create a habitus, a zeitgeist or a figured world that is constantly changing. I have chosen to use the concept of figured world to encapsulate the culture that neoliberalism and mangerialism, along with the humans and materials, combine to create in my world of work. In my figured world managers and workers act out the roles assigned to them, and they use the frames given to (imposed upon/actively accepted) them

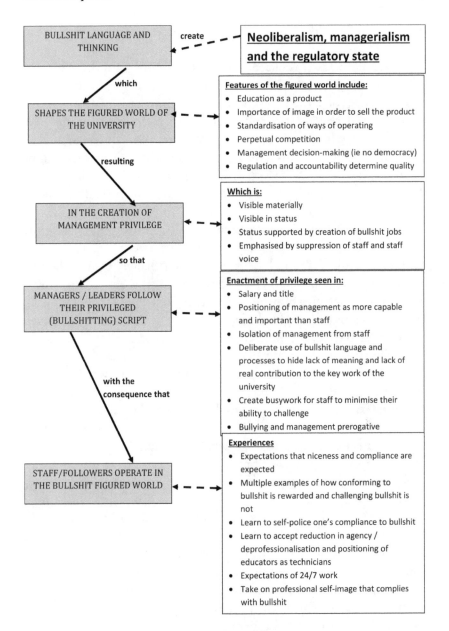

Figure 1. Conceptual framing

in this figured world to understand their experiences and to then act in that world.

Figured worlds as a concept was introduced by Holland, Lachicotte, Skinner, and Cain (1998). Figured worlds consist of the socially constructed understandings of participants that define for them how they are expected to operate in that world (Cleland & Durning, 2019), what value they have to that world, and thus their identity (personal and/or professional) in that world. Figured worlds have a history which helps people determine their social status relative to each other, the roles they should play, and the ways in which they should interpret the behaviours of others (Pennington & Prater, 2016).

The idea is that roles, expectations and identity apply specifically to each figured world, so that as people move between different figured worlds their role, value and identity may well change, as indeed, these might also change through time. For example, in the world of work a person might perceive him/herself as inferior, incompetent and unimportant, whereas in the figured world of a sporting club where that person functions as a coach, a completely different perception of role, value and identity may be held. This links to the importance placed on context in post humanism in understanding the relationships between elements of assemblages (Fox & Alldred, 2017). Day to day experiences are interpreted by participants in the figured world based on their perception of their role, status and professional identity. Each of these are learned through interacting in the figured world, learning through relationships with not only other humans but materials present in that world, and interpreting experiences through the lens of their previous understandings and interactions.

The way in which we operate in each figured world, according to a Deleuzian perspective, then becomes automatic (Moss, 2019), in that we become habituated to ways of operating and cease to think critically. Often, we do not step outside the scripts that form our figured world unless something completely different happens that disrupt our habitual patterns. Deleuze (1995; Deleuze & Guattari, 1987) calls these challenges 'lines of flight' as distinct from the automatic, habitual thinking patterns imposed through our figured world (rigid lines).

We know that the language we use shapes not only what we say, but how we think (Jones & Hoskins, 2016). Vygotsky himself identified how the language we use in interacting with children becomes internalised as their thought (Vygotsky, 1962). As Davies (2005, p. 2) states so succinctly: 'discourses colonize us.' Language thus shapes reality within an organisation: 'the reality of an organisation is it's linguistic reality' (Banerjee, 2003, p. 3). In the figured world of my university workplace the language of bullshit is used to communicate the values, priorities and expectations associated with the figured world created by neoliberal managerialism. Over 10 years ago Davies (2005, p. 1) warned that the adoption of neoliberal, managerial language in higher education risked changing the world of education: 'the discourse through which we, not quite out of choice and not quite out of necessity, make judgements, form desires, make the world into a particular kind of (neoliberal) place.' I argue that this has indeed happened, and that bullshit language has become the language of the dominant discourse, neoliberal managerialism, and thus it has gained (or been given) the power to shape the perceptions, understandings and behaviours of those working in that world, both managers and workers. Bullshit language is therefore of crucial importance in the operation of the figured world. Bhat (2017, p. 36) argues: 'language as a powerful tool is used to shape and re-shape realities, beliefs, and worldviews and how it acts as a complete tool of social control, conditioned by "other" non-linguistic parts of society.' This is exactly the position in which I place bullshit language. It shapes perceptions of the world through the words considered acceptable to describe it and thus speaks reality into existence (Lloro-Bidart, 2017).

In line with Deleuzian thinking, bullshit language offers the ability to appear to be conveying complex and important information, whilst in fact, skating across the surface and hiding a complete lack of critical thinking. Bullshit language obscures the fact that speakers are simply repeating the habituated patterns that form the figured world and their roles within that world (Deleuze's rigid lines). Bullshit language comes from an unthinking acceptance (Klikauer & Tabassum, 2019) of the figured world, its roles, values, practices and beliefs, as created by those in power, to the point where those participating in this world and using this language are unable to think outside the box it has created for them

(Kenway, Boden, & Fahey, 2015). Quite simply, bullshit language enables us to act out of habit without thinking (Davis, 2017). 'Bullshit is unavoidable when circumstances require someone to talk without knowing what he is talking about' (Frankfurt, 2005, p. 63). In that sense, bullshit language can create a sense of security: one is not required to think about difficult issues but rather reduce them to a few bullshit words and phrases (Spicer, 2018) so we can 'focus on comfortable, yet ultimately empty solutions' (p. 14).

In his original presentation of bullshit language, Frankfurt (2005) argued that bullshit was used deliberately by those in power in order to deceive. However, I posit the unthinking acceptance of the values, beliefs, practices and roles in the figured world seduces people into recycling the bullshit in a fashion rather like that described by Safdar and van de Vijver (2019) in relation to acculturation. Here what I mean by acculturation is the process that occurs when people with differing beliefs and values participate together in a figured world and gradually take on the beliefs, values and practices of that figured world, changing from beings holding those they brought into the figured world to beings who simply reflect those of that world. Bullshit language fulfils this function in the neoliberal managerial world. It speaks into existence a set of values, beliefs, practices and roles that are accepted by many of those operating in the figured world, and who, in the process of accepting and acting, validate and reproduce them without conscious or critical thought.

There is reason for reproducing bullshit language. A hierarchy of acceptable words exists in the figured world so that those who wish to prosper in that world have to learn the right words to use to clearly demonstrate their belonging to the elite group (Gaztambide-Fernández, 2011), in my context, managers. This bullshit language results in further privileging the elite (managers) as it serves to justify their status (after all, one who is fluent in management bullshit language clearly deserves a position in the elite). Those who are not fluent in bullshit language are positioned as undeserving outsiders (they could have chosen to learn the right language but have not done so; an individual failing) and any systemic barriers (the disadvantages associated with child bearing and rearing, moving from a very different higher education system overseas, for example) are ignored.

Bullshit language not only confirms for the elite their deserving status, but hides the privilege that placed them in the elite group in the first place.

Managerial privilege is established and maintained in the figured world by bullshit language and the values and actions that arise from it. Workers' identities are shaped by the way they are positioned in bullshit communications, in material differences not only in their work space but in rewards for the work they do, and by the way they are treated (including the bullshit language justifications provided for such treatment). As Freire (1973) identified many years ago, oppression becomes internalised and thus part of one's identity is shaped by the privileged whose positions of power are only maintained when workers accept their oppression as the natural and appropriate order of things. Questioning that privilege is therefore a dangerous activity, and quickly identified as unprofessional, unnecessary and, at the political level, traitorous.

Methodology

The focus of this book is an examination of my experiences in the figured world of one university in Australia. Thus, the most appropriate way to gather the data is to use autoethnography. In some ways autoethnography can be thought of as a story that contains theory. Stories themselves are important; they are the 'means by which we navigate the world. They allow us to interpret its complex and contradictory signals' (Monbiot, 2019, p. 1.26). However, the theory in autoethnography is the essential element that changes the story from a simple narrative of what we are, and what happened, to something that moves away from the ordinary into what might be (Holman Jones, 2016). Theory provides the vehicle that supports interpretation, viewing through a critical lens which makes change possible. Taking a classic interpretivist ontology, Ceisel and Salvo (2018, p. 308) argue that autoethnography uses the personal to enable an understanding of the 'collective nature of existence.' Bell, Canham, Dutta, and Fernández (2019, p. 8) explain:

> Autoethnography renders experience as a source of knowledge, liberation and power because it is anchored in undoing the hegemonic logics of knowledge and being, along with the discourses and mechanisms of a disembodied research practice.

Autoethnography 'constitutes a fantastic chance for conducting rich, insightful, and thick' (Winkler, 2018, p. 236) research, and it is important to ensure that the study on myself does not subsume the aim to study the figured world in which I participate. This requires a balancing act be performed between the 'auto' and the 'ethno' elements of the methodology which can be difficult. Roth (2009) considers too strong an emphasis on the 'auto' is unethical as it demeans the culture (in this study the figured world) in which we are embedded. In contrast, too strong an emphasis on the 'ethno' shifts the approach into classic ethnography. Ellis (2004) suggests this balance is best achieved by shifting the gaze back and forwards multiple times between these two poles.

Autoethnography requires me to use language to talk about my experiences. In a classic social constructivist approach, the language I use is thought to act upon the material world and thus shape that world. The material world is thought to be passive in this process. In contract, in a flat ontology, as proposed by Deleuze and Guattari (1987), the language used and the material elements of the world are of equal importance in having impact on the world. Thus the tool of language which I use to create my data can be used whilst at the same time I can recognise the importance of the material world; whilst language structures how I present my world, it does not have to solely define it (as explained by Jagger, 2015). Relating this to my conceptual framework, I identify the ideology of neoliberalism, and its enactment in organisations through managerialism presents impact in a hierarchical fashion. However, within my organisation I think about my experiences and the assemblages I present in my autoethnographic narratives using Deleuze and Guattari's notion of the equality of affect of both the human (and the language of myself as the human) and material elements. This means that my reflections of my experiences are represented as events and as explained by Fox and Alldred (2018, p. 193) these events consist of: 'the endless cascade of material interactions of both nature and culture that together produce the world.' In this sense, my stories form part of the social practice of my work, and in telling them I am renegotiating my own understandings, fully aware of the tensions, discontinuities and editing involved, in a manner similar to that discussed in Humle and Pedersen (2015).

The presence of emotions in autoethnography is part of the tradition of this methodology. Denzin (1997) argues that bringing emotion to the stories in a way that others can share the feeling is a key element of successful autoethnography. Autoethnographic studies including emotions are called evocative autoethnography and L. Anderson (2006, p. 374) expresses concern that this approach runs the risk of 'eclipsing other visions of what autoethnography can be and of obscuring the ways in which it may fit productively in other traditions of social inquiry' such as realism. To address this, he introduces another form of autoethnography he calls analytical autoethnography, aiming to be 'consistent with qualitative inquiry rooted in traditional symbolic interactionism' (p. 375). Anderson's position is that autoethnography should not only describe but it should explain through developing theoretical understandings that move beyond the data. It is this element that forms the greatest disjunction between evocative and analytical autoethnography; however, Winkler (2018) suggests that these forms should not be perceived as two separate ends of a binary continuum, but rather that we should value multiple voices and multiple approaches. Another voice in this debate is that of Holman Jones (2016) who, rather than joining the evocative vs analytic argument, proposed another form of autoethnography she calls critical. She argues theory is written into the story through language: 'I weave my language into and through the language of theory, citing the work either in the main text or in endnotes' (p.234). This approach, she claims, creates a bridge between the writing from the body (evocative autoethnography) and writing from above (analytical autoethnography); in effect '(b)ridging analysis and action' (p.234). In this study I am using Holman Jones' discussion of critical autoethnography to guide me so that I can incorporate theory into the stories and use this to help me explore not only my experiences, but the potentials for resistance. At the same time, I am aware of the need to include emotions and materiality in my data to make my reflections as rich as I possibly can. Autoethnography, used in this way, facilitates the naming of '"private" pain in a deliberate move towards healing and imagining a decolonial reality' (Bell et al., 2019, p. 7).

Data

In creating my stories, I am calling on a number of resources that cover the time period 1992–2019. I have material artefacts such as online documents (my own and others, publicly available) and my own files and notes. There are emails (e.g. publicly available mails sent out to the entire university community and available on a website that does not require a university login to access) and my notes hand written in notebooks. However, a significant element pulling these disparate materials together is my memory. Chang (2008) argues that there are risks in relying on memory in autoethnographical work. Winkler (2018) suggests that memory provides a form of soft data and that other more tangible data (such as a researcher journal, notes) might be considered as hard data and that both have their value. Despite the different values assigned by different researchers to memory data, it remains a recognised form of autoethnographical data and Chang (2013), in a later work, has acknowledged the value of recall in generating data. Winkler (2018, p. 238) concludes that a demand for hard data is 'probably violating the ontological and epistemological assumptions of autoethnographic research.' However, this does not invalidate the use of hard data, it simply positions soft data as equally useful and recognises that it is not appropriate to require all soft data to be validated by hard data; memories can stand on their own.

Stories written from memory and supplemented by material artefacts where possible are a form of reflective writing. Barad (2007) talks about reflection as an inner mental activity aimed at enhancing one's understanding of the world and one's position in that world. In contrast, critical reflection can be seen as enabling the transition from thinking about the world to acting critically within it (Bozalek & Zembylas, 2017). This kind of thinking should then enable one to make choices about one's behaviour, but of course, it is important to remember that choices are influenced by position in the world, and the extent to which one is subject to the power of others. Critical thinking is thus a tool used to help identify what is happening and why so that one's behaviour is guided by thought.

Rigour

Loh (2013) suggests that those doing any other form of research but posi-
tivist are pushing the boundaries of what many consider the norm. This
is particularly evident in social policy where it is considered randomised control trials are the 'gold standard' of evidence needed to justify
intervention programmes (Mannell & Davis, 2019). Despite this, many
researchers are engaging in non-traditional forms of research, of which
autoethnography is one. As in any form of research, determining the
work is valid and truthful is important but such judgements have to be
made within the parameters of the research ontology and epistemology.
Many years ago, Lincoln and Guba (1985) identified standards for qualitative work that required a demonstration that the research met a range
of standards including: credibility (internal validity), transferability (external validity), dependability (reliability) and confirmability (object-
ivity). The equivalent to Lincoln and Guba's criteria in narrative research
are trustworthiness, narrative truth, verisimilitude and utility (Loh, 2013).
If the research cannot be trusted then there is little point in undertaking
it. Loh refers back to Lincoln and Guba's criteria for trustworthiness as
the most respected in the sector. Of the techniques recommended to establish trustworthiness I have undertaken:

1. Prolonged engagement – I use data from the past 27 years of my
   working life in universities;
2. Triangulation – with research literature, and other forms of publicly available data;
3. Peer validation – multiple interactions with others, conference
   presentations, online feedback, peer consultations;
4. Thick description – including not just what happened, but the
   context, emotions and materiality dimensions;
5. Dependability audit – checking the stories against the available
   hard data;
6. Confirmability audit – checking that the data supports the
   interpretations.

The criteria, verisimilitude, requires that the work rings true to others; other university employees across the country ought to read the work and feel that there are parallels with their own experiences. My previous work in this area (Sims, 2019a, 2019b) indicates that this is indeed the case.

Loh (2013)'s final criteria is that of utility: utility questions if the research is useful. I can only make that judgement at the end of the process when I evaluate the usefulness of strategies of resistance arising from the process. Others may make their own judgements of the usefulness of the process and the final outcomes.

Analysis

In traditional qualitative work data are perceived as passive, something that awaits action in order to be transformed into interpretation. In other words, data require manipulation by the researcher in order to have meaning. In doing so, the researcher imposes some kind of structure or framework on the data and it is this framework that is expected to represent the underlying reality, or shared understanding that potentially leads to change. The conceptual framework, provided in Figure 1, serves this purpose, creating a lens through which the data is manipulated in order to guide interpretation.

In contrast post-structuralist research removes the focus of interpretation from data analysis:

> We suggest that data may manifest as an event in which data, theories, writing, thinking, research, researchers, participants, past, future, present, and body-mind-material are entangled and inseparable. (Koro-Ljungberg, MacLure, & Ulmer, 2018, p. 479)

Here data is inseparable from analysis and the researcher is intimately embedded in the assemblage. As identified in my ontology and epistemology section, I am moving between these positions, creating my own path that enables me to entangle the data I generate from my own stories with the thinking and writing that presents these stories and the conceptual framework I use to structure their presentation. In this way I attempt to present a messy, constantly changing, unbounded conglomeration of experiences in a linear fashion as suits the sequential requirements of written language.

In this process the standard techniques to establish data credibility and rigour are themselves incorporated into the data assemblage. For example, triangulation with the literature and rich description of context become part of the stories and therefore part of the data, rather than standing separate in easily identifiable sections of the writing. Thus, in presenting the stories simultaneously with the interpretation/analysis of the stories, I am creating a narrative that assembles the various components (events, emotions, materiality) into a messy whole that illustrates the inter-relations between these elements as they occurred within my specific contexts. Analysis therefore is part of the story creation, and whilst guided by the conceptual framework, will illustrate the relationality of the different elements.

Ethics

In autoethnography my story is not only mine. It is inevitable that others will be included in different stories so it is important that these others are considered and treated ethically (Winkler, 2018). Whilst autoethnography is not normally a form of research that requires approval of any formal ethics committee (Stahlke Wall, 2016) it is important that I recognise the rights of any person involved in any of my stories. One school of thought suggests that all those involved in any of the stories should be contacted and asked to provide informed consent, however it is more generally recognised that this is impractical and may even be counter-productive. In my case, I believe this approach would indeed be counter-productive. Instead, the concept of relational ethics as introduced by Ellis (2007) is a useful guide to appropriate ethical behaviour. This means that others must be treated with respect and dignity, and I must ensure nothing written about another person is something about which I would be embarrassed to show to that person. I also need to be clear that I am telling my stories and not impute intentions or feelings onto other people: these are not their stories but mine and I can only talk about my experiences, my feelings and my understandings. Others are only included in terms of their observable behaviours, and only those observable behaviours that have low or no risk of identifying them.

Ensuring anonymity is important, particularly given my identity and the names of the universities in which I have worked are public knowledge. To this end I am helped by the multitude of changes occurring at my current university in recent years. These include a restructure that added faculties to create new reporting lines: previously Heads of Schools reported directly to the Deputy Vice Chancellor. Heads of School were supported by Deputy Heads. As a result of the restructure we now have Discipline Cluster Leaders, reporting through Deputy Heads of School to Heads of School, who in return report through Associate Deans to Deputy Deans to Deans and ultimately to the Deputy Vice Chancellor. In my own school in recent years there have been a multiplicity of Deputy Heads and Heads/Acting Heads so that in the past three years I can count eight different Heads/Acting Heads, four different Deans, along with other changes in deputy and associate personnel. In a 10-year period I have had over 10 different direct supervisors. In my role as a case manager for the union (National Tertiary Education Union – NTEU) I have interacted with people in all of these different layers across the university (up to and including the Vice Chancellor, the Chancellor and Counsellors), so my engagement is not limited to my own faculty/school. I have also interacted with managers, deputy managers and other levels of management within the various directorates that sit outside faculties and schools. In this work I will refer to all of these positions simply as 'managers/management' to make it impossible to identify to which level, and to which area they belong (anyone in a supervisory role over other staff is classified as a manager). In addition, my stories will span a period of 27 years and I will not locate the stories in any particular time period (unless that is necessary, and in doing so I am not identifying anyone who is not already publicly associated with the story I am telling), making it even more difficult to locate any particular person except for myself. The only exception to this is where the information is in the public domain, and in cases such as this I will provide the relevant reference to support the public identification. Where I consider it necessary to be sure of protecting anonymity, I will tell composite stories and these will not be flagged as such. I will use generic gender-free English names (to avoid any possibility of assuming the ethnic background of anyone included in a story) for all involved in my stories and where I need to use pronouns and possessives will use the s/he and his/her forms so that there is nothing in the stories that might hint at gender, age or ethnicity.

Summary

I do not locate this work squarely within any specific epistemology and ontology but rather claim I am informed by key elements of interpretivism, social constructivism but I acknowledge I am also influenced by ideas from posthumanism and new materialism. Because I am not 'doing' this book by one particular approach I thought it important to explain the conceptual framing in some detail. This is illustrated in Figure 1. I argue that neoliberalism, as an ideology, is enacted in organisations through managerialism. This combination creates a figured world within my organisation that defines the values, beliefs and practices that are acceptable and valued, and conversely, those that are not. Thus in order to be successful in this figured world, people have to take on roles where they profess to hold certain values and beliefs, and demonstrate that they do so by their actions: in other words the figured world creates roles into which people need to fit if they are to be seen as successful. In this world those in management (who maintain their managerial positions) have to take on the management role as defined in the figured world; to not do so is a clear indication that the person does not fit (does not deserve a place in the elite group).

Language plays a crucial part in the figured world: in effect language speaks the figured world into existence. The language used in this world is bullshit language: language that is designed to convey the beliefs and values reified in the figured world. However, this language, whilst often sounding profound, actually covers an almost complete lack of meaning. Thus, managers can sound profound and learned. Those receiving the bullshit language, and charged with implementing what it says in a way conspicuous for its lack of clarity, are identified as failures when the outcomes are (unsurprisingly) not as managers expected.

Speaking bullshit language fluently cements a position in the managerial group and serves to obscure the lack of critical thought behind standardised, habitual practices in the figured world. Managers gain confidence through having the right words to say and rarely seek to delve into any deeper meaning (partly because such a deeper meaning rarely exists). Difficult problems become easy to solve when the solutions are meaningless words. The fact that these meaningless words rarely have good outcomes can be blamed on the inefficiency of the listeners (i.e. the workers).

In undertaking this study, I combine a number of data sources. Key amongst these are my reflections, mainly undertaken by memory but some were written contemporaneously with events as they occurred (had I thought in the past that I would write this book I would have written many more contemporaneously). These reflections from memory are supported by a range of different hard data sources including:

- case files (private and anonymised where used),
- emails (both public and private),
- documents,
- notes taken contemporaneously from meetings, discussions, fora and other relevant events.

Where others are involved in any of the reflections, I have taken great care to ensure they cannot be identified. Reflections cover the years 1992–2019, they can involve anyone at any level across the university, and they cover a period of significant change where there have been multiple changes in management. I use gender-free English names for people other than myself, and use non-gender identifying pronouns and possessives to obscure gender, age and ethnicity (I do wish someone would invent a gender-neutral pronoun and possessive for the English language).

The following chapters each address the key themes in the study. I begin by examining the figured world of universities. This involves an examination of the way in which bullshit language has shaped the figured world and the roles inhabitants of that world are required to play in order to participate.

CHAPTER 3

The figured world of the organisation

The courses in which I teach were up for accreditation. We had to work through the Australian Children's Early Childhood Quality Authority (ACECQA) guidelines of what content we have to ensure students gain before graduation. ACECQA is a national body, established to administer the National Quality Framework for early childhood education and care. ACECQA not only accredits early childhood services (ensuring compliance with the National Quality Standard and the various laws related to this enacted in each state and territory) but accredits the courses offered through tertiary training institutions that meet their standards to be recognised as a qualification in early education and care/early childhood teaching. This is aimed not only at improving quality in the sector nationally, but ensuring staff can transfer anywhere in the country and have their qualification recognised. This is a very different situation than in the early days when graduates were only accredited at state level, and, therefore, had to apply for recognition of qualifications obtained everywhere else. I well remember the work involved in sitting on the WA qualifications committee and having to assess qualifications from other states and other countries before their holders could work in WA. At one point early on in the process, all my team received an email identifying the learning outcomes that must be covered in the course. Each of these learning outcomes needed to be mapped onto unit content and on to the assessments in that unit. There also had to be an overall course mapping to ensure some kind of equality across the entire course (ideally we should not all be teaching the same sets of learning outcomes in all our units!). There were an awful lot of them and several members of the team, relatively new to this process, were rather freaked out at the thought of this work. We all got together and talked about it, huddled around a laptop in our dedicated teaching space (surrounded with shelves of toys, drawing implements and dolls – an image that felt so different than the dry paperwork we were trying to work our way through). Whilst I tried very hard to be supportive and positive, part of me was laughing inside. I have been through similar processes too many times to count and I cannot remember a single time when this mapping exercise, no matter how seriously I took it at the time, made any difference at all to the content of what I taught and the way I assessed it. At the end of our joint discussion we all went away to map our individual units. The mapping required we identify the ACECQA learning outcomes by number (1.2, 1.2, etc.). We had to break our content down into weeks (at this point we are teaching 12 weeks a trimester, at a later point this changed to eight so the mapping had to be re-done), identify the topic and subtopics for each week, and map the ACECQA outcomes, and our own unit learning outcomes to each week. This not only required an in-depth knowledge of the content, it also requires a cross-check with the online learning platform (Moodle) to ensure that the weekly topics were indeed as they were presented in Moodle, or at least, as I intended them to be when I have updated Moodle. Occasionally I had to dip into the Topic Notes on Moodle and the readings to make sure that a particular ACECQA element is actually where I thought it was. It's quite a laborious process and I was continually having to go back to the master list of ACECQA outcomes to check the numbers, even occasionally getting my numbering mixed up between the ACECQA learning outcomes and my unit learning outcomes. I work on a laptop so having parallel screens open simultaneously does not work for me – if I do this the print is too small to read. Thus swapping screens involves minimizing one and clicking on the other. Then I had to remember numbers when I click back to the form screen. As each day progressed and I got tired I found myself making mistakes – one would think it a simple task to remember a two- to three-digit number for the few seconds it takes to click from one screen to another but my brain feels overloaded and the more I got frustrated, the more mistakes I made. Finally I got this done for each of my units and turned to the next page of the forms. Now I had to do the same thing but map the ACECQA outcomes and my learning outcomes for each unit onto each of the assessments. Again, I had to check my assessments actually enabled me to claim that each of the claimed ACECQA learning outcomes, and each of my unit learning outcomes, are actually assessed so that I can legitimately claim that a student passing the unit has demonstrated an acceptable level of understanding in the identified learning outcomes. I find this kind of work incredibly boring and laborious and it is so easy to get lost in the detail. I plodded my way through it and finished my forms with a sigh of relief, having taken several hours on each form (at this point I was doing forms for four undergraduate units so this is equivalent to half a week's full-time work). I have discovered nothing in this exercise that suggested to me that I need to change anything in my units. The balance of content I offer seems about right to me and the assessments are giving students the right balance of opportunities to demonstrate their possession of the required knowledge. I might make some slight clarifications to the unit learning outcomes, just in terms of the wording for the next cycle, but otherwise things are okay. Some other poor person in our school received all our forms and did whatever magic is required. I forget the whole process. Not too long after, we all got another email requiring us to map the university's graduate outcomes into our units, content and assessments. I gritted my teeth. At least this is a reasonably sized list of learning outcomes. I really do not believe these are useful or realistic so I took this task relatively lightly, added my mapping to the forms for each of the units and sent them back – about a day's full-time equivalent work. Many months later the team receive an email from the poor person whose job it is to spend all day, every day, on accreditation of our courses (what a job – I have huge admiration for people who can take on such a job and not go nuts as I would were I in that position). It appears that the mapping has either been done to the wrong criteria, or that the criteria have been amended (I am still not absolutely clear about this) and we were all sent back our forms and asked to check them. I searched in vain for the master list I had used the first time but could not find it anywhere on my laptop. It never ceases to amaze me how I believe I save everything in sensible, easily findable places, yet when I need something like this I can never find it. I felt incredibly frustrated because this had come at a really busy time, and I resented the time I was going to have to dedicate to the task, time that I could not use to get more of my marking out of the way. Of course this task had to be done urgently, but so did my marking which policy requires to be turned around in much the same timeframe. I ended up printing the new master list (having saved it in what I hope is a findable place this time) and tried to work through each unit, checking the numbering used in the unit against the new master list. However, printing the master list was not as good an idea as it seemed at the time. I am not clicking between screens, but my desk is not exactly neat and tidy and there was very little room to put the master-sheet near me in a place where I could actually read it. In addition, my glasses are designed for exactly the distance between my eyes and the screen and the printed list was outside this distance no matter how I tried place it. I found myself peering at it, shoulders tight and neck stretched. Occasionally I remembered posture and re-adjusted but then sunk into the job only to tense up again. Given the time lapse since I did this mapping last time, I found myself having to go back and check stuff on Moodle again and again as I did the first time. So despite the printed list, I was clicking from one screen to another. I felt a growing sense of outrage at this use of my time, and all the time I am doing this I felt the marking calling me. Students were beginning to query when they were getting their marks back and I was aware that unit evaluations can be influenced by a delay here. I also resented every second I had to take time away from both the mapping and the marking I was desperately seeking to complete in order to answer student queries about when they were getting their marks; at the same time I was supposed to be teaching and going onto Moodle several times a day to scaffold learning. It was so hard to remain polite and to respond with careful and thoughtful scaffolding when my brain felt like it wanted to burst with impossible deadlines. At the same time I was aware that I needed to support the person doing the accreditation work because there were external deadlines associated with this work as well and the person was required to meet these. This re-mapping was not done with the same sense of commitment as the first mapping, and I got it done over a period of several days (about 12 hours total) interspersed with marking and sent it back. Again, we had a period of quiet at our end (not for the person doing the work pulling it altogether but that work is hidden from me, thank goodness). Some months later, we all got another email informing us that in NSW there are now a set of Professional Standards for Teachers against which our courses needed to be mapped in order for our graduates to be accredited as teachers. There is some confusion as to whether early childhood teachers are included in this process. For months we were unsure and I watched my colleagues in primary and secondary education struggle with this process and avert my eyes so that I could pretend it is not going to happen to us. I heard colleagues complaining that the standards do not align with others standards against which they are required to map their courses, and I shuddered to think of the mis-matches between standards designed for primary and secondary teachers with those we would want for early childhood teachers. There are times hiding one's head in the sand is a smart survival strategy and I won't allow myself to even think about this new mapping until such times as I am coerced into doing it.

The higher education market

In Chapter 1 I touched on the debate around the marketisation of higher education. Now it is appropriate to extend that argument further, because what I claim we are seeing in the kind of work I have described above is attempts by government, following a neoliberal policy framework, to identify and standardise the product being sold. The product in this case is a qualification (supported by state funding through the student support scheme, HECS) that enables its holder to work as a trained professional in a particular sector. In my case, in early childhood, a national body, external to higher education providers and government funded, is responsible for identifying what knowledge and skills are required for someone to be recognised as an accredited early childhood teacher. Pre-service courses providing the relevant education are therefore required to demonstrate how they can be sure graduates have that required knowledge and skillset.

The language of marketing requires that qualifications are positioned as a product, and as a product, they must be standard so that where one obtains a qualification is less important that the actual qualification itself. This ensures that those who have purchased the product can legitimately seek employment across the sector, nationally, and thus feel that they have been granted value for their money. Those delivering the product must therefore be controlled so that the product does not deviate significantly from year to year nor from institution to institution. The ideal academic, therefore, should be positioned as part of a standardised production line, each person contributing towards an externally defined, and internally controlled, part of a standardised whole (Watts, 2017).

As a consequence:

> Neoliberal policy reduces universities to the production of instrumental knowledge premised upon economic values that ignores the social and political role of universities, renders them as just another transnational corporation out to make a profit. (Blackmore, 2015, p. 193)

Having created this version of the world, where teaching becomes part of a production line, and universities simply become corporations designed to make a profit from selling their wares, the language of business bullshit operates to obscure the inadequacies of the market model as it operates in higher education. Bullshit language creates and validates a form of life for those in higher education organisations. As Bourassa (2019, p. 8) argues:

> In short, the control of educational life is central to the reproduction and maintenance of neoliberal capitalism. In the political economy of educational life briefly described above, this means that some forms of educational life are harnessed and sapped, and others enclosed and arrested.

As I work through this chapter, I will identify the ways in which bullshit language harnesses some forms of educational life and encloses others. In terms of my conceptual framework then, this chapter addresses the heavily shaded box, Features of the Figured World in Figure 2.

Student centred learning

In an ideal world good-quality teaching in higher education could be positioned as explained by the University of Aberdeen (2016, p. 6):

> Truth is never given in advance; it is rather a horizon of attainment that ever exceeds our reach. It is not therefore available for transmission, as is implied by models that measure teaching and learning by the achievement of predetermined outcomes. There can be no such outcomes, beyond training in skills of so superficial a nature

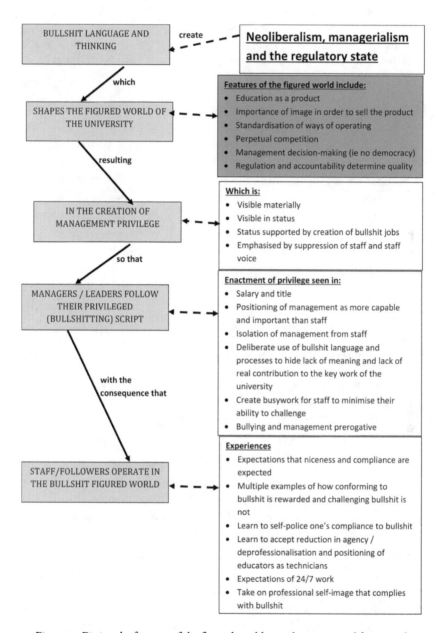

Figure 2. Fitting the features of the figured world into the conceptual framework

that their transfer can be achieved and assessed through the completion of tick-box exercises. Teaching is not about the transmission of pre-existent knowledge; it is about guiding students in journeys of growth and self-discovery that they necessarily undertake together.

Given one of the most important 'products' a university is supposed to offer is a quality learning experience (few universities do not have some reference to student experience in their strategic plans: the UNE 2016–2020 Strategic Plan frames this in terms of delivery of an outstanding student experience – <https://www.une.edu.au/about-une/executive/vice-chancellor/strategic-plan/strategic-plan-2016-2020>), it would be logical to assume that university policies and processes would actively support ways of teaching that are known to best facilitate student learning. Unfortunately that is often not the case: 'It is insulting and abusive when universities charge academics with providing a flawless service to students, and then chisel away at the conditions and hours which would permit it to be accomplished' (Morrish, 2018, p. 2). Staff at the University of Aberdeen (2016, p. 6) claim:

> In succumbing to the market-driven rhetoric of teaching and learning with its calculus of milestones and measurable outcomes, and in divorcing research as the production of new knowledge from teaching as its dissemination, the university has abandoned its educational mission. Learning has been reduced to the smooth and painless acquisition of information, so that students can obtain good grades with minimal effort and leave as satisfied customers.

Most research on teaching and learning identifies concerns around the traditional model of university teaching: that of transmitting information, usually via a lecture, to large groups of students (the larger the better, as this lowers the cost per student). The online equivalent to this is preloaded material for students to read through, sometimes (and increasingly required) accompanied by pre-recorded lectures. Traditionally, the lecture is supported by tutorials where smaller groups of students gather together with an academic staff member at regular, scheduled times throughout the teaching period, and discuss the material delivered in lectures. In the UNE Academic and ELC Teaching Staff Collective Agreement 2014–2017, a tutorial is defined as: 'a supplementary form of education delivery where matters already covered elsewhere in a course are discussed, clarified or elaborated. A tutorial is conducted in a small group to enable effective student participation' (Schedule 2, Definitions, b). Tutorials as they traditionally operate in Australia, are based on a constructivist approach to teaching and learning, the assumption being that jointly exploring the content will help each student link the new knowledge to their existing understandings, and, in professional courses, explore how this might then be applied in their practice. In my experience, as funding cuts continue to squeeze universities, tutorial sizes have increased. When I first began teaching in the university sector in Australia my tutorial groups did not exceed 15 students. More recent experiences had me taking up to 40 students in a tutorial. True constructivism, as I understand it, requires the funds of knowledge each student brings into the learning situation to be recognised by the teacher, who then constructs individualized learning opportunities to build on these existing strengths. Whilst this is difficult in a class of 15 students, it is totally impossible in a class of 40 students. The larger the class size, the more likely it is that tutorials will consist of pre-prepared exercises that require students to work through specific content, discuss pre-identified issues, and share their discussions in the hope that exposure to different perspectives might help them broaden their thinking. The academic's role morphs from exploring each student's understanding in depth and building on this foundation, to facilitating class discussions that enable the more vocal students to share their ideas.

The online equivalent to tutorial discussions is, in my experience, particularly contentious. As an academic, I strongly support the concept of one-to-one scaffolding of student learning through forums on the online platform (Moodle in my recent experience). I argue that the questions students ask provide an opportunity to scaffold their learning and that other students in the unit can then explore these interactions and share in the learning. In my experience, other students often join a discussion thread so that it is possible to build a collaborative, though asynchronous, discussion. Thus, I argue that answering questions on Moodle is a fundamental element of constructivist teaching that is more demanding of the academic than fronting up to a large tutorial group and facilitating the group as they work through pre-prepared activities. Scaffolding learning individually online through forum discussions requires the academic to have an in-depth understanding of the unit content, and an understanding of the context in which students are working in order to help translate ideas into practice. Added to this is an ability to read what is often not written in the questions, to figure out what students are thinking. In theoretical terms, this involves identifying where the student's Zone of Proximal Development – ZPD – begins in order to shape a response that moves the student through their ZPD to not just build on the student's strengths, but to work towards the required learning outcomes. (I use the term ZPD in the manner first identified by Vygotsky, 1962.) These do not always match, and in an ideal world, should not be required to do so. In addition to doing this for the student who asked the question, it is then necessary to expand the answer to try and target the ZPDs of other students who respond in the discussion thread, and, at the same time, provide sufficient challenges in an attempt to prompt other students to join in the discussion.

This all sounds good in principle, however the point I am working towards is that such an approach is not recognised as teaching in my context, and perhaps not across the entire sector (Watts, 2017). It is on public record that management in the School of Education at UNE unilaterally decided that answering questions on Moodle forums did not constitute teaching, nor did this represent the online equivalent form of a tutorial. Therefore, it was appropriate to no longer pay casual academics teaching rates to scaffold students' learning online, but rather pay the Other Academic Activity Rate (OAA) which is a third of the tutorial rate.[1] Consequently, any unit in the School of Education 'taught' by a casual academic (and there are currently many as, in my area alone, at one point we were more than 50 per cent short-staffed) is not paid to be 'taught.' Students enrolled in those units can only expect to receive 40 minutes per trimester of a casual academics' time to support their learning by not teaching them. At the same time as

---

[1]   The case in the Fair Work Commission, heard by Commissioner Johns: [2019] FWC 1171 National Tertiary Education Industry Union v University of New England (C2018/4494). Decision document Fair Work Act 2009 s.739 – Dispute resolution.

this is happening the university continues to boast about its five-star student satisfaction rating[2] so that the uninformed member of public looking at UNE would be led to expect the quality of teaching being offered is of a very high standard.

This five-star student satisfaction rating is presumably obtained through good-quality teaching, elements of which are identified by UNE's policy document *Teaching and Learning Expectations for Staff and Students* (<https://policies.une.edu.au/document/view-current.php?id=422>). This document uses words such as scholarly dialogue and flexible when talking about teaching. Scholarly dialogue, one assumes, is offered in tutorials but it also states alternative learning technologies can be used. I argue the non-synchronous interactions between academic staff and students in Moodle fora are examples of scholarly debates and therefore contribute towards the university's five-star rating (and off-campus students have a large say in generating this rating as they are a larger cohort than on-campus students). The necessity for on-campus and online students to be offered a similar level of quality in their learning is reinforced by the Higher Education Standards Framework (Threshold Standards) 2015 (Annexure C, Sections: 1.1–1.5) (<https://www.legislation.gov.au/Details/F2015L01639>). Thus, my opinion, reinforced by UNE's policy and Australian government legislation, is that in pursuing an argument in the Fair Work Commission that positioned online engagement with students as not 'teaching', management were operating counter to their own best interests in maintaining the five-star rating.

To me, this disjunction between claims of offering a high-class student experience, and the harsh economic reality (that cuts costs to the point where short staffing and cuts to casual academic pay rates make it impossible to teach students well), represents a classic example of bullshit. Neoliberal managerialism emphasizes the importance of cost containment (meaning less resources applied to enable quality teaching), but

2   As of July 2019 the UNE home page boldly proclaims: 'The stars are out. UNE is the only Australian public university awarded the maximum 5 stars for Overall Experience 13 years in a row.'

at the same time the importance of marketing the high-quality product on offer. Management are able to reconcile these two extremes quite comfortably; acknowledging in the Commission that the work undertaken by casual academics meant they were 'required to discuss, guide, and engage' with students online (Decision document, p.22, point 47; the very activities defined in the Agreement as constituting a tutorial), but simultaneously arguing that this work does not meet the remaining elements of the definition of tutorial. Given 'a bullshitter will say what works to get the outcome they want, and care little whether it's true or not' (Ball, 2017, p. 6) this seems to me to be a classic example of bullshit in operation. Those using bullshit in this example appeared to me to be perfectly competent in holding contradictory positions together in their minds, able to argue for a position that put quality teaching significantly at risk, whilst at the same time, touting the importance of a quality student experience. Internalisation of the bullshit scripts created by neoliberal managerialism thus not only allows the holder to speak 'mis-representation, half-truths and outrageous lies' (Ball, 2017, p. 5) but obscures the completely different meanings spoken in different contexts to different audiences.

My argument here is that bullshit language is the tool that enabled managers, in this example, to hold two contradictory (and one would think mutually exclusive) positions simultaneously, and feel sufficiently comfortable in doing so as to make sworn affidavits in the Fair Work Commission in pursuit of their aim of reducing pay for workers. Bullshit language functioned to justify management actions that can only reduce the quality of teaching and learning. Unfortunately, by the time this is reflected in the data gathered in the national graduate student survey (see <https://www.qilt.edu.au/about-this-site/graduate-satisfaction>) many of those involved are likely to have left the university, and those remaining are most likely to attribute the decline in student satisfaction as the fault of the academics who taught them. In other words, bullshit language justifies not only attacks on the ability of academics to deliver good-quality teaching, but will then squarely locate the blame for declining results on the very academics struggling with higher and higher workloads imposed upon them.

Standardisation

Watts (2017) argues that in many instances senior managers are completely unable to define what learning actually is, and this lack of understanding makes it easier for them to impose neoliberal managerial strategies on those who do have that understanding. This imposition is usually enacted through the development of policies and procedures designed to standardise the 'product', and standardised tools to measure compliance and performance. These standardised policies, procedures and tools are foundational to neoliberal managerialism, but anathema to academics attempting to offer quality learning experiences for students.

> The seductive power of these instruments relies on the fact that they contribute to transform complex and multi-dimensional educational realities into numerical categories, and to construct the perception that deep educational problems (such as inequalities or quality issues) can be addressed by setting up predefined patterns of conduct, measuring actors' performance, and distributing incentives accordingly. (Verger, Fontdevila, & Parcerisa, 2019, p. 264)

Along with these policies, procedures and tools comes the bullshit language used to justify their existence. This language focuses on quality. There are a multiplicity of quality rankings now used that are supposed to demonstrate to the market which university is better than another based on a set of numeric categories (for example, The World Top Universities – see <https://www.topuniversities.com/student-info/choosing-university/worlds-top-100-universities>; The Times Higher Education rankings – see <https://www.timeshighereducation.com/world-university-rankings>; and a range of other rankings summarized at <http://www.shanghairanking.com/resources.html>). However, there is considerable debate as to exactly what is measured in producing these rankings and Watts (2017, p. 171) argues:

> it is quite unclear what relationship the various rankings of universities has to do with whatever is meant or defined as 'quality' ... quality in higher education has nothing much to do with metrics of student satisfaction, research output, or even 'quality

of teaching' however that is defined and measured ... It has everything to do with
being a 'sandstone' university in Australia.

The difficulty of identifying and measuring quality at a national level is
reflected inside universities in the challenges associated with establishing
what can be measured in relation to teaching and learning and thus used
to define quality. Again, the challenge is addressed in the neoliberal managerial university by imposing standardisation on what can be standardised, and enforcing compliance to these standards, and ignoring anything
that can't be standardised or measured; that is, the intangible elements of
teaching (Emma Rowe, 2019). For academics this generally means standardisation of elements of their work that are not particularly important
or meaningful, and dismissal of elements of their work that actually contribute to high-quality interactions with students.

I have taught off campus students for over 25 years and in all of that
time there have been occasional attempts made to require me to insert my
teaching materials into some kind of a template. The evolution of online
learning platforms has accelerated those attempts. Whilst I acknowledge
it is useful for students to have some consistency across units of study in
terms of where key elements can be found (that all the explanations for
each assignment can be found under an assignment tile for example, or that
e-reserve readings can all be accessed through the same tile in all units),
I continue to strongly resist suggestions that I should post, in every unit
I teach, a weekly lecture (the numbers don't add up – given an online student is supposed to get 40 minutes per trimester of my time, and lectures
are usually 50 minutes, how I am supposed to create and post 8 weeks
of lectures without 'volunteering' unrecognised time has never yet been
explained to me), or that I should record every on-campus tutorial class
and put it on Moodle for off-campus students to view. Lectures and tutorials, posted online, are easy to identify and their presence/absence is easy
to measure. Their presence is assumed by management to mean that the
teaching offered is of good quality. As discussed above, research suggests the
exact opposite. The bullshit language around quality fails to recognise the
reality of these requirements, and simply positions me as non-compliant
(and thus a poor teacher by definition).

This leads me to consider the standardised definition of a good teacher. For several decades now, the student experience questionnaire (called different names in different organisations, but by this I mean the survey completed by students at the end of each unit of study designed supposedly to evaluate the quality of the unit of study and of the academic(s) delivering it) has been used across the sector in Australia as a tool aimed at improving quality (see <https://www.une.edu.au/about-une/executive/deputy-vice-chancellor/academic-quality/surveys/unit-and-teaching-evaluation-surveys> for information on the UNE surveys). At UNE a certain (failing) score will generate a requirement for a Unit Action Plan where the academic is expected to complete a proforma for the supervisor identifying what elements will be changed the next time the unit is delivered. Such plans, to those generating them, appear to be subsequently lost in a black hole as no further feedback is offered and there is no recognition of improvements. Despite this, I have personally heard a Promotion Committee refuse to promote someone on the grounds of poor teaching because this person had, in the past, been required to provide a Unit Action Plan (neither do I remember in the Committee discussions anyone looking to see what changes had been made as a result of the Action Plan and the impact of these). In more recent years I have seen academics who achieved the highest possible score (a perfect five) being required to complete a Unit Action Plan because of their attrition rates (which are uniformly high in trimester three, and often high in particular courses because of the particular student cohorts involved). The point of this example is that despite standardised measures suggesting someone is an excellent teacher (scoring the perfect five) that person is still positioned as a failure because of attrition rates, of which much of the underlying contributing factors are outside the control of the academic concerned.

Watts (2017) argues that these student evaluations of teaching are responsible for decreasing the intellectual challenge in units of study. Academics, he argues, aware of how important scores are to their careers, seek to improve scores by making their units easier for students, by requiring less intellectual effort both in the readings provided, and in the assignments set. As a consequence, whilst scores might indicate highly successful units, the reality is that students graduate with less knowledge, understanding and competence. I have seen a staff member instructed to modify an assignment based on a complaint that the assignment was too difficult from one student in an evaluation that was completed by over 50 students, 49 of whom had no complaints about the assignments. Clearly, keeping students happy is considered of more importance than challenging them to learn.

Basically, as Hil (2012) argues, academics feel driven to modify their teaching so that they maximize their scores on these evaluation tools, so that in effect, the evaluation tools create a standard definition of what is good-quality teaching and learning. This is unfortunate as a range of literature demonstrates that there is little correlation between scores on student teaching evaluations and the actual quality of student learning (Joint Task Force on Teaching Assessment and Evaluation, 2019). Despite this, my effectiveness as a teacher is evaluated every time I teach, using questions such as:

- 'The learning outcomes of this unit were made clear to me' (they are provided, I cannot make students read them, nor can I require them to look at the marking rubrics that evaluate their assignments against the learning outcomes for the unit);
- 'I received constructive feedback on my work' (this one doesn't sound too unfair on the surface because yes, feedback should be constructive; however, comments often indicate a difference in perspective as to what is constructive – 'to improve I recommend that you ....' is apparently not constructive according to several comments, nor is the identification of plagiarism accompanied by an explanation of where the student can find resources about how to avoid it);
- 'The overall amount of work required of me for this unit was appropriate' (this is a judgement call – my content is defined by an external accrediting agency. In the past few years I have had to condense that content from 13 to 12 to eight teaching weeks without losing any content and with students still meeting the same learning outcomes). This is an element I consistently score badly on. The way to improve my scores is to dumb down my units – require students to do less reading each week, and make the assignments easier. This is not a strategy that will improve the quality of students completing my units, though it may well improve my student satisfaction scores and even the overall graduate experience survey scores.

Along with standardisation of what constitutes good-quality teaching, is the associated pressure I have already identified, to make my units easier; easier for the students (who might reward me with good teaching evaluations) but also survive-able for me. My teaching load has consistently increased over the years so the kinds of assignments I used to require 20 years ago are impossible for me to manage now. I remember one unit (a final year, final semester unit) where I had students design, based on theory and a survey of a real community, an intervention programme of their choice. Several students, on graduation, actually located employment that enabled them to put their programme into action. In terms of the learning opportunities offered to the students, this was an excellent assignment but marking it took a lot of time; several hours per assignment for around 50 students. I am now expected to mark all of a student's work for one trimester in an hour. With 2 assignments per unit, I have to divide my time fairly across both assignments, and to mark over 100 students per trimester. This 100 hours of marking a trimester (over two and a half weeks full time in an eight-week teaching trimester just to mark, not to teach, nor offer pastoral support nor to engage in any other teaching related activity) does not reflect reality. Few academics I know, me included, can actually complete marking in this time without making major modifications to assignments. This means we either spend time marking that is not recognised (and therefore we should be achieving other goals in that time but are not) or we amend assessments to make it possible. Standardised, computer-marked quizzes are a popular choice here because, apart from the time taken to set them up, they can then be completely computer-controlled. Removing traditional tertiary assessment staples such as essays and reports, and replacing them with computer-marked quizzes is seen across the sector as a rational response to increased teaching loads (Manathunga & Bottrell, 2019a; Watts, 2017). These are much less able to give students practice at developing and supporting an argument, but are effective in determining recall of specific content.

Along with the increasing standardisation of forms of assessment prompted as survival strategies to manage student evaluations and increased workload, is the increasing standardisation around how many assessments can be required, and when they are required. For example the UNE Assessment Procedures (<https://policies.une.edu.au/document/view-current.php?id=290>) require more than one assessment per unit, and that these assessments should be different forms (e.g. a quiz and a report, not two essays) and that one should be offered early in the trimester. The document identifies we are not allowed to have a 100 per cent exam as a unit assessment. No assessment can be less than 30 per cent or more than 60 per cent of the total unit mark and selected response tasks (e.g. multi-choice questions) cannot be more than 70 per cent of the total unit mark. Participation can be no more than 15 per cent, and peer assessment no more than 10 per cent unless the latter is subsequently marked by an academic. We are not allowed to allocate any marks for attendance. Word limits are imposed: basic level units are allowed up to 5,000 words in assessments, 200 to 400 level units are allowed up to 6,000 words; and 500 level and higher are allowed up to 7,500 words. A two-hour exam is identified as equivalent to 2,000 words. I consistently field complaints from students that they cannot convey the information they want to in their assignments within the word limits and whilst part of me is in sympathy with them, the other part has to say stick to the essentials, identify the most important elements. Along with Raaper (2019), I feel increasingly constrained and have reached a place where I do not believe my assessments offer the best possible learning opportunities for students; they do however offer the best possible learning opportunities within the constraints imposed on me.

Again, what we are seeing here is the tool used to measure 'quality' is responsible for changing what academics do, and thus changes what is positioned as good quality. Quality is increasingly identified as compliance to standardised requirements, and these requirements are themselves, limited to what is measurable. A quality unit has pre-recorded lectures and tutorials. It does not matter what students are learning; what matters is that particular elements are present. It does not matter that research does not identify these elements as good quality; what matters is that academics comply and provide these elements. Given the language of bullshit positions these as good-quality teaching, academics are coerced into believing this is the case, because to not comply positions us as poor teachers, a position that can significantly impact on our employment and career. The risk in complying is, of course, that we perform in ways that do not fit comfortably with our own professional image of ourselves.

Audit culture/accountability

Standardisation goes hand in hand with the requirement for staff to demonstrate they meet the standards (accountability), and the reification of an audit culture that demands we are accountable for everything we do. These demands for accountability, for justifying everything we do, are often experienced by staff as intrusive (Connell, 2019a), so that academics send more and more of their time each day demonstrating to managers what they are doing, rather than having time to actually do it (Watts, 2017). For example, in my early years as an academic I would simply go to a conference, and if I wanted university funds to help me, would pop my head around the Head of School's door to get approval and sign a piece of paper to acknowledge that the conference, and my work there, was legitimate. These days I have to:

1. Email my direct supervisor with information on the conference, my role in it, an assurance that my teaching duties (even in my non-teaching times) are covered in my absence, and the name of the person covering these for me;
2. Go online and complete the online travel form which requires me to:
   a. attach my supervisor's email approval from step 1,
   b. Identify what I am doing and where I am doing it for each day I am away,
   c. Identify for each day if the day is university business, weekend or private time (note the university imposes its own limits, which are less than Australian Tax Office limits, on how much private time (annual leave) we are allowed to add into an overseas trip, even when I am paying the entire cost of the trip

myself – many of my colleagues simply take annual leave to attend conferences as it is just not worth the bother of fighting this one),

   d. Identify the costs associated with each element of the travel: fares, meals, taxis, conference registration, trains, busses, incidentals, etc.,

   e. Identify who is paying each of these costs (e.g. myself seeking reimbursement, myself not seeking reimbursement, etc.),

   f. Identify the cost code to be charged for each element if it is charged to the university,

   g. Identify who is covering for each required element of my job: teaching, admin role if relevant (e.g. Team Leader, Course Co-ordinator, etc.),

   h. Identify who in the university is required to approve;

3. The electronic form, once submitted then goes to my supervisor (who initially gave me permission via email in Step 1) for approval;

4. It then travels through the hierarchy to:

   a. The travel agents if they are a required part of the booking,

   b. If they are, they load the travel arrangements and the form comes back to me for approval, then I resubmit to my supervisor,

   c. Then from my supervisor to the HoS, Dean, and if international travel to PDVC – each of these is most likely handled by the associated Administrative Assistant who may refer on but I don't know for sure. Certainly, any questions I am asked come from the relevant Administrative Assistant.

Including someone from the travel agency, there are now at least five people who are involved in the chain of approval for me to travel to an international conference, presumably each one of them checking that I have filled in the form correctly, all the correct boxes are ticked and that my itinerary clearly establishes I am working, not going on an overseas jaunt for the fun of it. Adding their time to the time I have taken to complete all the steps (can be several hours for me) indicates that a substantial amount of organisational time is taken in this compliance requirement, time that each of us in the chain could probably spend much more productively working on the university's core business. Accompanying this is a range of unwritten rules that are a trap for the unwary and falling into any of these traps can increase the time spent in attempting to gain approval significantly. If I exceed the university's private time limit, I have to tick a box to indicate I am aware that I am required to pay a proportion of the costs (even when I have already identified I have or will pay all the costs). If I have an annual leave day on a Friday and on a Monday then the four days (Friday to Monday) count as private time. In comparison if I work on either a Friday or a Monday or both, then the weekend is not counted towards my private time allowance. Exceeding my allowance for private time increases the complexity of the application substantially and I have to spend a great deal more time explaining why this amount of private time is justified and is not taking away from the work I will be undertaking.

Manathunga and Bottrell (2019a) claim that increasing accountability requirements take time away from the work academics traditionally performed in universities. One academic has recently developed a petition calling for a national inquiry 'to streamline/improve research ethics and governance in Australia' (<https://www.thepetitionsite.com/en-gb/981/617/971/we-need-a-national-inquiry-to-streamlineimprove-research-ethics-and-governance-in-australia/?taf_id=63138497&cid=twitter&utm_campaign=website&utm_source=sendgrid.com&utm_medium=email>) claiming that millions of dollars are wasted by excessive compliance demands (Matchett, 2019). From my perspective, this is certainly the case. I recently took on the role of Team Leader (having avoided any form of management for the past decade I figured this small role in my team was not a move towards the dark side but simply a level of organisation I could do to support my team). This role focuses particularly on staffing; making sure each member of the team has a full workload over the academic year, supporting them in seeking and appointing casual academic staff to help them when they are overloaded, and appointing and supervising casual academic staff working in units that do not have any ongoing staff involvement (in terms of ongoing staff we have been over 50 per cent down for some time). We all know that student enrolments fluctuate, and given students can enrol pretty much all the time (though not quite), we are often still taking enrolments into the first weeks of trimester. Staff workloads need to be organised as much as possible well before the beginning of trimester (so they can prepare their teaching materials, assessments and their time) meaning the identification of workloads can sometimes be rather a guessing game. Contracts for casual staff can take weeks to be formalised (where I can, I send them in really early but there are occasions when Moodle units open and there is no academic engaged to teach). Official student numbers are sent to me on a semi-regular basis and each time I am required to update our team workload spreadsheet to check that every ongoing staff member still has a full load. I then have to re-adjust the numbers of students our casual academic staff are teaching and marking (woe betide me if a casual staff member has a contract for more students than needed) and send in the relevant contract request forms for each. I have to re-do all the contract requests when the official withdrawal period ends (in Australia once we are past the official withdrawal date, students are charged even if they later withdraw, and the government funds the university for that student's place). As we come into each trimester, I could easily spend 40 to 50 hours working on the spreadsheet, contacting potential casual academics, completing the contract request forms, liaising with ongoing staff to determine their intentions for subsequent trimesters, checking contracts as they are issued, and briefing new casual academics. We operate three trimesters so this workload is duplicated three times, though not to quite the same intensity as we progress through the year as I am not projecting so far ahead given workloads are calculated on a calendar year. I am lucky because we have a pool of casual academics who have worked with us for some time. Other teams in the school do not, so I am aware that other team leaders may spend much more time seeking casual academics, checking their credentials and supporting them as they learn our systems and ways of doing things. All of this is essential work but the time I take to perform it now is probably 10 times longer than the time I took in the past when I was staffing my discipline (which was larger with more staff) 20 years ago. This is time for which I receive minimal recognition (a teaching release of 8 students per year). The large amount of unrecognised time takes time away from the other elements of the core academic work I am expected to perform, and these expectations are not adjusted to take into account this compliance workload.

Thus, the audit culture in which I work makes it difficult to achieve the academic elements of my work that I am expected to produce. One consequence of this is that many university staff work much longer hours than the standard working week for which they are paid. For example, the 2015 workload survey undertaken by the NTEU (National Tertiary Education Union, 2017) showed that across Australia, the average working week for academics was 50.7 hours (they are paid for a 37.5-hour week), and professional staff worked an extra 5.7 hours a week unpaid overtime. This work overload impacts on staff health and wellbeing. A recent study in the UK showed that occupational health referrals of staff increased by 64 per cent between 2009 and 2015, whilst counselling referrals increased by 77 per cent. Women staff in particular were more vulnerable with 60 per cent of the occupational health, and 70 per cent of the counselling referrals being women (Morrish, 2019). In Australia, around half of university employees can be identified as at risk for mental health problems compared to a 19 per cent risk rate in the general population (Watts, 2017). Watts argues: 'The tertiary-education system would come to a rapid halt if all those who were entitled to it, decided to take stress leave' (p. 251).

What I find particularly frustrating in this kind of audit culture is what appear to be different standards applied to staff compared to managers. I am not alone in this. Graeber (2019, p. 170) writes: 'in the lower echelons, competence and efficiency actually do seem to be the reigning values; the higher one goes up the ladder, the less true this appears to be.' Take Special Study Leave (SSP) in my context for example. SSP is a period of time where we are released from all other job obligations except for the research project or professional experience we have identified as the target of the special leave. SSP is positioned as a privilege, not a right; that means we can apply for SSP every 3 years and whilst the duration of our service since the last SSP defines the amount to which we are entitled, there are no guarantees that any academic will be successful in their application. I am aware of colleagues who put forward competitive applications but who were told by a manager that, rather than the 6 months to which they were each entitled at that time, they were only going to be given three months and they must take at least two weeks annual leave in that three months, meaning the actual study leave period was two and a half months. Not to worry, they were told, you have not lost the remaining amount to which you were entitled; you can claim that next time you apply for SSP. The reason given for this restricted time period was that these staff could not be spared; they were required to teach their full annual teaching load in the calendar year in which they took SSP (other areas of the university at that time were calculating teaching requirements on a pro rata basis, not requiring the full load to be covered) and therefore there just was not enough time in the year for them to take a longer period of SSP. I remember at the time trying to fight this on their behalf on the grounds of equity but to no avail. Sometime later one of the managers involved in imposing this restricted SSP was him/herself granted study leave for six months.

I find it particularly interesting to examine the language used when this particular grant of SSP was announced publicly. The projects this manager was undertaking were outlined in some detail. Many reading the communication interpreted the explanation as a need to justify the special leave, particularly given that it came with no prior warning to staff outside the management group, and was not associated with a specific SSP round. This SSP was claimed to be long deferred but the projects named were all current. The manager was praised for the careful thought that had gone into the replacement people for this person's various responsibilities, but this requirement was standard for all those applying for SSP under this manager's authority. I believe this illustrates that the standards of accountability to which staff were held by this manager were not, in turn, applied to this manager. The language used to communicate this decision was, I argue, deliberately phrased to obscure the inequity in both the taking of leave and the duration of leave whilst positioning this manager as undertaking something tremendously desirable. This is bullshit language at its finest; obscuring inequities and defining the ways in which recipients of the communication are meant to interpret this behaviour.

There are consequences to these kinds of inequities. The growing gap between management and staff makes it difficult, if not impossible, for management to be aware of the extent of the anger and disillusionment staff feel when they perceive these inequities (Connell, 2019a). Staff are much more likely to attempt to flaunt accountability regimes that they perceive as inequitably applied and this leads to managers' feeling more and more distrustful of staff (Connell, 2019b) and a lack of understanding as to why staff compliance is tokenistic rather than heartfelt exacerbates this distrust. Increasing levels of managerial distrust tend to result in even more onerous accountability regimes in attempts to ensure compliance, which act to further disempower staff and build feelings of resentment.

Agency

Spicer (2018, p. 18) writes that a neoliberal, managerial organisation:

> focuses more of its efforts on talking about doing things ... increasing amounts of its time showing that it has complied with regulation and less of its time to actually serving the public ... stakeholders gradually realise the organisation does not seem to be doing its core task at all, or if it is, it is being done poorly by under-resourced and under-experienced people.

Both the state and its 'domestic economic actors are increasingly disciplined by neoliberal market norms' (Carroll & Jarvis, 2015, p. 298). Demonstrating compliance to these requires a multiplicity of policies and procedures, and in recent years, rules in place of policies (I am told that rules are preferable to policies because rules can be legally enforced, whereas policies cannot). The reality is, so many of these exist within organisations that it is impossible for any worker (or manager) to be conversant with them all. For example, a count on the UNE policies website (<https://policies.une.edu.au/masterlist.php> as of 5 July 2019) identified 64 policies, 62 rules, 106 procedures, 31 guidelines (plus an additional 17 guidelines specific to the on-campus child care centre), eight protocols, four codes, three plans, two statements, one each of an annex, schedule, standing order, MOU, expectations, charter, and framework, and 32 terms of reference; a total of 328 documents specifying how things should be done and by whom.

Meeting the requirements of all these policies, procedures and rules requires 'armies of boxtickers' (Graeber, 2019, p. 160) to check that the right things are being done at the right times and by the right people. This creates an administrative overlay pressing down upon those doing the core work of the university resulting in:

> *a sense that the pleasurable aspects of one's calling, such as thinking, were not really what one is being paid for; they were better seen as occasional indulgences one is granted in recognition of one's real work, which is largely about filling out forms. (Graeber, 2019, p. 217)*

As a consequence, academics now feel they are losing control of their work (Taberner, 2018), and have 'a sense that not much seems to make sense anymore' (Watts, 2017, p. 224). Managers engage in deliberate attacks to destroy the traditional autonomy of academics using 'psychodynamically charged exercises of violence' (p. 274) to do so. This is evident in a number of different ways.

Firstly there is a concentrated effort around Australia to exclude university staff from governance roles (J. Ross, 2019b). In particular, J. Ross (2019a) claims that around Australia University Councils or Senates are now mainly filled by people from the corporate sector whereas elected university staff have been reduced to 14 per cent, compared to a 17 per cent presence 10 years ago. The increasing presence of corporate members is linked to the perception that universities will function better if they are run like businesses, and who best to provide that expertise than those employed in the business/corporate sector. Staff are increasingly positioned as biased, as having a conflict of interest, as was indeed, the allegation made when the Chancellor of UNE attempted to remove me from the University Council (for public reports see <https://www.theaustralian.com.au/higher-education/nteu-branch-chief-margaret-sims-take-une-to-court-over-council/news-story/2224f18d3a15b00f581551fb309afoca> and <https://www.theaustralian.com.au/higher-education/une-backs-down-on-sims-case/news-story/985241635150f013bb18663ff82ab2f7>). Despite having no evidence of any form of misconduct, the allegation was that I would be unable to separate my legal responsibilities as a member of the Council from my interests as President of the UNE Branch of the NTEU. To me, this signals clearly the perception that staff are not to be trusted; with the concomitant position that they therefore must require intensive, intrusive supervision to ensure they are doing the right thing.

Reflecting on another management attack, Hayes (2019) talks about the growing incidence of 'groupthink' in the higher education sector where staff are expected to adopt the values of their organisation and not engage in criticism. Staff are expected to accept the conditions imposed upon them, and the values and practices espoused by management. This includes the expectation that staff should simply comply with the mind-numbing compliance work imposed upon them because presumably that 'is a form of moral self-discipline that makes you a better person' (Graeber, 2019, p. 94). Ever growing compliance demands and ever decreasing agency associated with the growing punitive audit culture in universities attack staff feelings of professionalism and work to silence staff (Bessant, 2015). Silencing staff voice then legitimizes management's claim that they are better positioned to make decisions; they have an overview that staff do not, and therefore their voices should be privileged.

Whilst compliance can be coerced, it can also be enticed through false rewards, with an emphasis on the need for staff to perform as part of the team for the benefit of all (a 'good' staff member will work harder for the benefit of all). In other words, bullshit language is used to hide the exploitative nature of management demands, and instead position them as things staff should be doing for their own benefit. For example, in NSW the teacher accrediting bodies (NESA and AITSL) require education students to complete a Teaching Performance Assessment (TPA) before they graduate (see <https://www.aitsl.edu.au/deliver-ite-programs/teaching-performance-assessment>). Whilst this is compulsory, there are no resources allocated to the universities who need to do this, and that means there are no funds available to pay staff extra, nor to recognise this work in their teaching workload. Thus management need to persuade staff to take on additional work involving a minimum of a half day training, plus time for the actual marking (which I am told is substantial) and additional time for moderation across the staff engaged in this activity. Rather than counting as part of their annual teaching load, staff were told that they could count this work as part of their service to the university. Staff were informed that the Expert Advisory Group for this activity recommended that a team of academics across different disciplines within the school should be involved in this activity. The inference I read from the tone of the 'request' is that staff should feel privileged to be part of this exercise, given that this 'service' to the university can be evidence to support a promotion application.

Management attacks on staff professionalism and agency (staff are positioned as untrustworthy) is again explained using the bullshit language of quality. It is important that staff fill out multiple forms because their managers need to know where they are for insurance purposes. At the height of one kind of stupidity, a manager insisted that people fill out a travel request to go from the university into town (a 5 minute drive) to undertake an organisational visit that was a core part of their teaching role. This was claimed to be a requirement of the university's insurers, not the manager's own misunderstanding of university policy and procedures. In another example, it is apparently important that supervisors, Heads of School, Associate Deans and even the PDVC look at unit evaluations to identify poorly performing staff/units so they can target their demands for improvement (as if a discussion with the immediate supervisor was not enough, we have to have at least 4 layers of management involved). Increasingly, managers appear to be acting as if their main aim is to break any possible resistance to their punitive directions, and to destroy any vestiges of previous collegial, autonomous academic culture (Kirkby & Reiger, 2015).

Summary

In the figured world of my university, neoliberal managerialism has created a culture that reifies the market, and the language and processes of marketization. As a consequence, I see students increasingly being positioned as consumers. As consumers, students are perceived as buying a product (a qualification) and their views around that product are considered important. Their voices (for example in unit evaluations) are valued more highly than those of staff.

Along with the priority placed on student voices is the perception that the product being sold should be standardised to ensure quality. At national level, standardisation is imposed through government and accrediting body regulations that define what ought to be taught, and what processes need to be in place at the institutional level to ensure quality. Within each university, standardisation is imposed through institutional rules, policies and procedures that define how students should be taught and how their knowledge should be assessed. Each of these layers of standardisation come with accompanying strategies for quality assurance, creating an audit culture where academic autonomy is severely compromised. Each of these layers uses the bullshit language of quality to justify the audit regimes imposed.

Both of these elements (student as consumer and standardisation/accountability) create a context where the pedagogy associated with high-quality teaching and learning is compromised. Measurement tools designed to ensure quality teaching and learning can only measure what is measurable (data such as attrition, student ratings of satisfaction), not what we know actually contributes to good-quality learning (such as academic-student interactions). Thus, quality is increasingly defined in terms of students' satisfaction ratings and attrition/retention data. In order to achieve good ratings, academics are learning to game the system; it is increasingly common to 'dumb down' units, to require less reading, less challenging assignments in return for better student ratings. The fact that such tactics do not benefit the students in the long term (nor their ultimate employers) is irrelevant because these short-term measures are all that matters. Again, the bullshit language of quality is used to hide the fact that, to improve student satisfaction, real quality is compromised, and 'false' quality is foregrounded.

Management reward those who achieve good scores on these irrelevant measurement tools, thus play a significant role in shaping teaching and learning (despite the fact that many have no teaching experience nor teaching qualification, and may not even be able to describe what good teaching and learning is about). In the need to demonstrate to increasingly audit-focused government and accrediting bodies that the 'product' being sold to students is one of good quality, management increasingly standardise all that they can in terms of their processes, working on the assumption that a one-size-fits-all approach will deliver the best possible product to the market. A lack of understanding of good-quality teaching and learning is actually beneficial here as it ensures little confusion gets in the way of a measurement tool.

Academic professionalism and autonomy are severely compromised in this process, as career progression, and even employment itself, is dependent on perceived success as defined by these measurement tools. Coupled with this compromise in academic work, is the increasingly onerous compliance audits that take so much time to complete. Many academics feel that they spend the majority of their time at work undertaking unnecessary and onerous compliance tasks and that the real work of an academic can only be squeezed into evenings and weekends, so that the average working week for staff is well in excess of the legal hours. As a consequence, there is a growing incidence of mental and physical health and wellbeing problems in the higher education workforce that combine with other factors in the figured world to creating a toxic culture. It is in this toxic culture that managers and staff experience their day-to-day working lives, and I will explore these in the following chapters.

CHAPTER 4

The invisibility of privilege

It's been two years since a colleague left a particular academic team (discipline) and has not yet been replaced. Over that time other team members have also left and not yet been replaced. Initially one position was advertised but no appointment was made. At this point, after the team had approved the job description and advertisement and sent these through the system, alterations were made that made it virtually impossible to recruit, and these new versions were used in the advertising and appointment process. Though team meetings members subsequently asked again and again what was happening with replacement staff, most of the time they received no answer at all. Once I remember being told that the replacement position had been approved and had been sent to HR for action, but nothing happened. Then the team were told there was going to be a school review: there was no particular reason given for this and it was not the time for the normal 5 yearly review. They were told that the review would be conducted by external panel members and that if they wanted to say anything to the panel they could come along to a school lunch. The panel would only meet outside of this event with those they selected, and surprise, surprise, that does not include any of this particular team. Now when the team ask about replacement positions they are told that these are on hold because of the school review. The review report is eventually submitted and after a time circulated around the school. Then the team are told they cannot have the replacement staff because the report is being considered by the PDVC. This takes several months. Hope fades for any chance of replacement staff for the new year so instead the team proceed to cover the necessary teaching with a (large) number of casual academics. Eventually they hear that one of the courses taught in their discipline is to be reviewed as it is deemed unviable – the only course recommended by the school review to go through this process which is somewhat puzzling as it is one of the largest and healthiest courses in the school (and a course that has to be reviewed as part of the regular external accreditation cycle, a cycle it completed some time ago and one in which the team is already gearing up to recommence in 6 months' time for a reaccreditation that is 18 months away). Now the team cannot get any replacement staff because the course is under review. This team has more casual academics teaching on their courses than they have ongoing staff. This has major implications for quality as there are a number of units that no one in the ongoing team have ever taught, and these units are not being updated when they are taught casually trimester after trimester, year after year. Payment for casual academics has been cut substantially and team members do not feel it appropriate or ethical to ask casual academics to do any more than simply teach the units as they are unless they can get approval for some additional hours for unit updating. So the team continue on, trimester after trimester, with few ongoing staff, expressing endless gratitude to the coterie of casual academics who hang in there with them trimester after trimester.

What frustrates me in this scenario is, at the same time as this team (and many others in the same area) is so seriously understaffed, I am seeing a plethora of professional staff positions being created. These are positions justified on the basis that we now have faculties, and that there needs to be a layer of faculty administration to support school administration. Some of these positions arise when school positions are changed to faculty level (okay, I can deal with that), but a number are new positions entirely, apparently necessary to support the increase in bureaucracy created by introducing another layer of management (i.e. faculties). I can no longer submit my ethics applications to the Ethics Committee, for example, they now have to go through a faculty level research officer (a professional staff position) who submits for me. When I have a PhD student ready to submit, I am supposed to send the thesis to the Associate Dean Research (via the relevant school academic who then sends it to the relevant faculty administrative person who sends it to the Associate Dean) to check before it is signed off as okay to submit (I don't – but it won't be sent out for examination until the Research Office receive the signed authority from the Associate Dean so my compliance is enforced). This is not just happening in my faculty, it is happening across the university. We now have a virtual campus (not that anyone around me has noticed it or had anything to do with it), so therefore we need a Programme Director for that campus. We even need a Sourcing and Category Manager who will 'drive strategic management of supplier relationships in order to optimise the university's profitability and competitive position' according to the job advertisement. We need an *Asset Compliance Coordinator who will be responsible for overseeing the maintenance, scheduling and reporting of asset-based compliance requirements to ensure regulatory obligations are satisfied.* We need a Content Optimization Officer. What we don't appear to need are academics to undertake the core work of teaching in a context where, for this team, there is over 50 per cent shortfall in FTE staff numbers. We are not alone in creating these (to the outsider), obscure roles. My colleague recently pointed me towards an advertisement for a 'Process Improvement Co-ordinator' at one university and a 'Course Management Advisor' at another. Obscure positions are not limited to the administrative side of universities: recently I saw an advertisement for two Professors in Strategy: when did strategy become an academic discipline, and when did it become so important that it requires two professors to work in the one university? Through all of this, many discipline teams struggle to hold their courses together with some degree of credibility. In the example above, given that half the units are taught by casual academics (who do a wonderful job with what is there) there will be a time when materials are so out of date that quality is severely impaired. At the same time, ongoing staff have determined they will not ask colleagues to pick up units they have never taught before, and use their research time to rewrite them, only to then hand over to someone else to teach. That is not fair. And despite all the new administrative positions, I do not experience an improvement in administration efficiency: both myself and colleagues are repeatedly being asked to resubmit forms that apparently have gotten lost in the system somewhere after leaving us. In my eyes there is an inequity where some sectors of the university (i.e. management) appear able to not only replace positions, but obtain new ones, whereas academics are forbidden (at major risk to quality) replacement staff. This inequity appears to go totally unrecognised thus indicating a complete absence of understanding of how privilege is playing out across the organisation. The final kicker happens when the team hear that proposal made in the school review to insert another level of management –departments within the school structure – has been approved and some of the Heads of Department positions will be externally advertised immediately. The thought of another layer of bureaucracy makes me shudder.

In this chapter I propose to examine the way privilege works in my figured world. In terms of my conceptual framework, the chapter addresses the darkly shaded box, the third down in the right hand column of Figure 3.

Management privilege and status

Growing managerialism and the associated accountability requirements have led to an inevitable increase in ' the total number of regulations, the total amount of paperwork and the total number of bureaucrats' (Graeber, 2015, p. 9) employed to manage these. The higher education system is no different in this respect to other organisations, both public and private. Smyth (2017, p. 144) writes:

> the 'exponential' growth in the size and cost of the 'university executive,' with its multi-million dollar salary bills and the associated out-of-touch academic empires that come with them, are completely out of control and serve no useful purpose whatsoever.

This is evident not just in Australia. In the United States of America (where Graeber, 2015, claims there is a particular fondness for bureaucracy) the number of administrative positions in universities grew 60 per cent in the years 1993 to 2009, whereas the number of tenured academics only grew 6 per cent in that time (Spicer, 2018). Data such as this lead Newfield (2018) to talk about 'administrative bloat' (p. 25), where the increase in administrative positions is 10 times greater than the increase in tenure-track professors. The publicly available annual reports from UNE (<https://www.une.edu.au/about-une/annual-reports>) also show a large increase in the number of professional (administrative) staff. For example, in 2006 the annual report identifies the university employed 492 academic staff (38.1 per cent of the total staffing complement) and 799 professional staff (61.9 per cent of the staffing complement). In 2017, academic staff numbers had grown to 531 (a decline of nearly 8 per cent to 30.1 per cent of the total staffing complement) whilst professional staff had grown to 1200 (68.1 per cent of the total staffing complement,

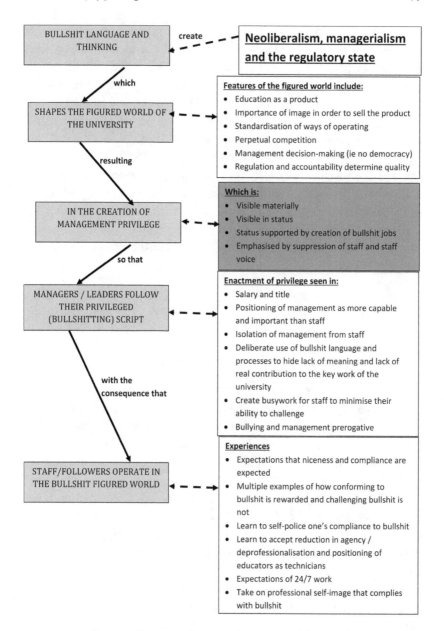

Figure 3. Fitting privilege into the conceptual framework

an increase of nearly 8 per cent – the remaining staff were employed in controlled entities and the annual report does not identify if they were academic or professional staff). Overall, the percentage of academics at Level E increased from 10.9 per cent to 12.1 per cent whilst the percentage of those appointed to the top 3 levels of the professional staff scale grew from 5.4 per cent to 23.5 per cent. Conversely, the percentage of academics at Level B changed from 43.2 per cent in 2006 to 36.5 per cent in the 2017 report, whilst percentages for professional staff at the lower levels (HEO 3 to HEO 5) declined from 78.1 per cent to 39.2 per cent. These figures demonstrate that the greatest increase in staffing over these years is not in the levels who are doing the actual work with students or supporting academics, but rather in the managerial ranks who have the responsibility to monitor those who are doing the core work of the university. Graeber (2019, p. 17) writes:

> the same period that saw the most ruthless application of speed-ups and downsizing in the blue-collar sector also brought a rapid multiplication of meaningless managerial and administrative posts in almost all large firms. It's as if businesses were endlessly trimming the fat on the shop floor and using the resulting savings to acquire even more unnecessary workers in the offices upstairs.

The bullshit language used to justify these increases talks about improvements in efficiency and therefore in quality. Management salaries are claimed to be set 'against comparable companies' and are justified because they result in 'the generation of long-term value for all stakeholders, namely shareholders, students and university partners' (a spokesperson for Unite quoted in Morgan, 2019, p. 2). At the local level, the ex-VC of UNE, Professor Annabelle Duncan, in her final interview with the local paper, the *Armidale Express Extra*, justified the faculty restructure (which introduced the new senior management positions of Deans, Deputy and Associate Deans at a cost of what I estimate to be $4–5 million annually for these positions alone) as bringing a 'more coherent management to the university' (Fuller, 2019, p. 3). It seems that good quality here is not about the learning experiences offered to students but about the detail and complexity of reporting the processes that control the work performed.

It is even more telling to examine the gender distribution of staff in the 2017 annual report. Of the academic staff, there were eight female (13.8 per cent) and 50 male (86.2 per cent) professors, but at the lower level (Level B) the ratio was reversed (107 women – 60.8 per cent; and 69 men – 39.2 per cent). Comparable figures in the 2006 annual report are 9 female professors (20.1 per cent) and 43 males (82.7 per cent), and at level B, 89 females (46.1 per cent) and 104 males (53.9 per cent). These figures demonstrate a disproportionate increase in male academics at the higher levels, and female academics at the lower levels of appointment. A similar pattern is seen in professional staff appointments. Despite having a female Vice Chancellor at this time, it is reported in the 2017 annual report that there are 11 women in the top three levels of professional staff appointments (39.3 per cent), and 17 men (60.7 per cent). In the bottom three levels of professional staff appointments there are 69 women (74.2 per cent) and 24 men (25.8 per cent). Comparable figures from the 2006 report are a little harder to judge as the reporting categories are not the same, however in the categories of Executive/Deans and Senior Managers, it is reported that there were five females (22.7 per cent) and 17 males (77.3 per cent). At the level of administrative/technical staff (which is reasonable to assume relates to the lower categories of employment) there were 283 women (62.1 per cent) and 173 males (37.9 per cent), again demonstrating a growing number of women in the lower levels over time and an increase of men in the higher appointment levels. This gender divide is relevant because the way power operates in patriarchy is intertwined with the operation of power in neoliberalism (Ortner, 2019) so that women in management positions are often positioned as status-incongruent (Smith, Rosenstein, Nikolov, & Chaney, 2019). In addition, operating as 'a handmaiden' of neoliberalism (Fraser, 2013), feminism has taken on board the neoliberal individualization imperative, legitimizing marketization and the retreat of the state from responsibility for citizen wellbeing. For women this has resulted in the need to work at least two shifts (the shift in paid employment and the shift in the family home and/or unpaid caring work), increasing levels of poverty when going it alone and increasing exploitation in lower paid positions; the latter clearly evident in the numbers reported above.

This positioning of women remains largely invisible, rendering the privilege of masculinity and management similarly invisible. The language of bullshit argues that such gender imbalances are not about any systemic discrimination, but rather about appointment of those who are worthy. The fact that women are generally judged worthy at lower levels and men are more worthy at higher levels is not, in bullshit language, about gender inequities, but rather about demonstrated competence. Appointments are focused on economic efficiency rather than on social justice (Jenkins, 2015). In reality, under neoliberal managerialism, the workforce is perceived as consisting of individuals who are 'race-less, gender-less and ageless and free to choose regardless of their material conditions' (Blackmore, 2019a, p. 177). The smaller number of women at higher levels, and the greater number of women in lower levels of appointment, are constructed, using bullshit language, as choices made by individual players. A woman can chose to remain childless and focus on building a career (as did Australia's ex-Prime Minister Julia Gillard, who was castigated as 'wooden' and lacking in empathy because of this choice; Anonmyous, 2011), or she can be positioned as lacking in professionalism and dedication to the employer because she chooses to take time away from her employment to become a mother (Gann, 2018). Either way, bullshit language claims that women make their choices freely and must therefore expect to experience the consequences. Demonstrating these inequities is positioned as nothing more than a snapshot of individuals' choices, and therefore not a social justice issue deserving systemic intervention.

Increasing masculinization of senior management means that successful leadership tends to become perceived as 'aggressive, competitive, self-centred and emotionally cold' and that any woman in a senior position must, in order to succeed, learn to 'manage like a man' (Connell, 2019a, p. 127). Power has thus become identified as masculinist (Schwartz, 2019). Different forms of leadership are increasingly overlooked, and those who operate by alternative forms are passed over for management roles, finding it increasingly difficult to gain promotion. I have read many promotion applications over the years in the figured world of universities, and believe that there are significant gender differences in the way people construct their arguments to establish their worthiness for promotions (and by gender differences, I do not mean to say that all men argue one way and all women another; rather than the masculinist focus is the one that is most successful, and this can be used by women as well as men). Those who are successful, I have found, tend to be those who make strong, aggressive claims: 'I achieved xyz as a member of Committee A', for example. More realistic claims ('as a member of Committee A, I contributed to the group achievement of xyz') are generally dismissed by Promotion Committees as not demonstrating acceptable levels of leadership. In reality, I argue, such claims are simply demonstrating either an unwillingness, or a lack of capacity, to use the language of bullshit to frame accomplishments. Thus, the masculinist management bullshit discourse used to speak to achievements renders the privileging invisible, as the focus remains on the claimed accomplishments rather than actual accomplishments. As discussed by Gaztambide-Fernández (2011), the use of bullshit here aims to communicate one's worthiness to belong in the elite, management group and render, in comparison, those who do not demonstrate capacity (or will) to use the bullshit language of belonging, as unworthy. Actual accomplishments fade in comparison with the 'correct' use of bullshit.

In this growing masculinization of successful leadership, privilege is invisible. The ability, or willingness, to use bullshit language to describe one's leadership style, and the identification of that style as the one and only way to function successfully in senior management roles, is underpinned by the neoliberal focus on individual responsibility. Success in operating in senior management requires adherence to a particular script defined in the figured world of neoliberal managerial universities as masculinist. Other scripts are not deemed worthy, and those who follow other scripts are thought to do so by their own choice, so by definition are not worthy of privilege. Privilege only accrues to those who follow the 'correct' script in the figured world. In other words, privilege accrues to those who make the choice to comply with the appropriate script, and who therefore deserve the rewards that accompany their compliance.

Accompanying group identification is the ignoring of advantages available through membership in the elite group, management. The language of bullshit is used to not only justify this positioning, but to hide the reality that others are blocked from any chance of joining this world of privilege

(Gaztambide-Fernández, 2011). This is what Hill (2004, p. 504) called the 'class war from above.' The possession of cultural, professional and economic capital accrued through membership of an elite group (i.e. management) creates a form of social inequity (Apple, 2017) that is reflected in widening gaps between those who are privileged and those who are not throughout much of the global north. Such imbalances of power become self-sustaining (Australian Council of Social Services & University of New South Wales, 2018), as it is certainly not in the interests of the elite to willingly relinquish their power to share more equitably with others. However, it is in their interests to minimise any challenges arising from 'the masses' in order to keep their position of privilege secure. The language of bullshit fulfils this function. Repeated exposure to bullshit language informing staff they are not worthy, because of the choices they have made for themselves, creates a self-fulfilling prophecy where staff internalise their unworthiness and cease to seek (or even desire) membership of the elite. It's easier to remain securely in the box in which one is placed than to challenge the scripts that locate one there.

Inequity

Inequity is an important element in the neoliberal market lexicon and neoliberal managerialism has successfully increased societal inequality to levels not seen for over 100 years (Watts, 2017). Increasing emphasis of the importance of maintaining the elite ('more opportunities for powerful business interests to exploit their position': Menadue, 2019, p. 1) and the decimation of the collective power of unionism have been major contributors to this increasing inequity. Maintenance is framed in bullshit language as the consequence of choices individuals make. This operates to make invisible the multitude of forces that maintain inequity. However, all those participating in the figured world learn their place and learn how they are expected to enact the role to which their position assigns them. A multitude of signals are used to identify and reinforce these placements in the figured world. These include elements of materiality, trust/mistrust and declining democracy.

Materiality

Status symbols have materiality. In the figured world of my university (and many others) this is reflected in the location and size of one's office and even the office furniture. For example, managers tend to have larger offices than other staff whereas some lower level staff (including lower level admin staff and contract academic staff) are placed in shared office spaces. At one point in my school all those with managerial roles were all moved into the top floor of one building so they were all together, creating a physical 'management space' that others rarely penetrated unless called to a manager's office.

Office accoutrements also reflect status. When I was first employed at UNE as Professor, I was told that I would be given a new desk, a new large meeting table and an office chair. The desk was 'relocated' before I arrived and I never found it, but I remain perfectly happy with a large meeting table as my desk so that the meeting space in my office can simply be a circle of chairs. Clearly the provision of a meeting table signalled that any meeting I would choose to have in my office should be conducted around a table that, by its very nature, closed me off from those with whom I was talking. I note that, across the campus, it is usual for managers to be provided with similar meeting tables in their offices, and suggest that the materiality of these tables is a signal of separation between those seated around the table. Most often these tables are not coffee table height but full table height (even when, in newer buildings, they are crammed into smaller office spaces) so provide a physical barrier between participants. When I attend a meeting in any of these rooms, I sometimes find it amusing to sit at the 'head' of the table rather than one of the sides. When I do this, I feel extremely uncomfortable, but I do it anyway to observe the reactions of others in the meeting. I have not yet been challenged when I do this, but it never fails to start the meeting with a general feeling of discomfort that, from my perceptions, appears to be shared by all those in the room.

I remember in all my years on Council (three two-year terms as elected academic staff representative) the Chancellor always sat at the head of the table, a clear signal of status. Whilst this is usually the case, I have attended other meetings (even some in the Council chamber) where the facilitator has chosen not to sit at the head of the table, but such occasions are rare and certainly did not happen in Council itself. Behind the Chancellor was a large window and the light coming in this window bounced off my glasses so that wherever I sat in the room I could not see his face clearly. Places next to the Chancellor around this large table were always occupied by senior managers: the VC, the Head of Legal and Governance and the Deputy Chancellor, for example. No one ever challenged for these places. I often used to wonder what would happen if someone did choose one of these places at the table and I have to confess I did not ever attempt to do so. Instead I sat towards the lower end of the table with my back to another large bank of windows. This meant that I struggled to see the screen of the Council i-pad I used for the meeting papers, but at least I could see the people on the other side of the table from me, but not the people further up the table on the same side as me. I sometimes experimented and sat directly at the foot of the table facing the Chancellor but the light coming in the window behind him prevented me from seeing clearly the other meeting participants on both sides of the table. Several requests to pull the curtains were refused on the grounds that others did not want to block out the light. When I sat at the side of the table there were several other people on my side between me and the Chancellor and it appeared that this made it difficult for the Chancellor to see me. There were many occasions when I wanted to speak that I not only had to raise my hand but I had to learn forward across the table to make a clear and open path between myself and the Chancellor and then remain in that position until I was acknowledged.

In many meeting rooms the chairs also speak a message through their materiality. In a number of spaces where I attend meetings, these chairs are fancier than those in our offices. They are softer, nicer colours, and often swing around and/or rock back and forth (in one meeting room they rock back so far that people are often taken unawares – something rather amusing to watch but uncomfortable for the unsuspecting). However, with few exceptions, they do not have an adjustable height (whereas my lower-class office chair does). This means that when I sit in them my feet do not touch the ground. This leaves me several options: I can have my feet dangling (which after a short time hurts my legs), I can sit forward (which means my back is not supported in the seat and that hurts after a short time), I can sometimes just reach the ground on my tip toes (which means my muscles cramp after a short while) or I can lean forward and flop my upper body on the table which shuffles me forward in the seat so I can reach the ground (but that looks like I am going to sleep lying on the table, and again this position hurts my back after a short while). The specific places where I encounter these chairs are interesting: in particular, around the Council table, and in the main meeting room for my school. In both these places, the ways that I am able to sit in the chairs are physical positions that place me in a child-like state: swinging my legs, anxiously propped forward, on tiptoes or lying on the table. It takes a conscious effort on my part not to allow that physical child-like state interfere with my thinking during the meeting. The process of monitoring how my physical position impacts on my thinking thus diverts some of my thinking capacity away from the issues being discussed.

In a similar manner Spicer (2018) discusses how bullshit language is used to divert thinking away from the real issues. Following this idea, I argue that the materiality of these chairs functions to divert my attention from the important matters of the meeting. This kind of diversion, according to Graeber (2019), aims to shift focus away from deep thinking to the kinds of surface thinking needed to support consumerism. I cease to engage in the debate, and instead, frown at anyone who prolongs the discomfort by asking questions, and focus my attention on getting out of the room as quickly as possible. The issues at hand quickly become of secondary importance to my desire to leave so I can be more physically comfortable and do the elements of my work that I want to do at that moment. The materiality of these chairs, despite my best intentions, does impact on my performance, my willingness to engage and my willingness to spend time thinking about the issues at hand. This kind of discomfort is rarely experienced by whoever is chairing the meeting. In the School meeting room (which is usually set up with rows of chairs and tables), the chair of the meeting (usually a manager) stands at the front of the room. In the Council room all members sit, but without exception the Chancellor has always been taller than me (in fact most Council members are taller than me – I cannot recall anyone who was not) therefore the discomfort

I experience in these chairs is not something others seem to experience. Thus, my discomfort remains invisible to managers (despite my verbal sharing) and the impact of that physical discomfort on my performance goes either unrecognised or is recognised and considered desirable and/or lacking in importance. Presumably if I chose to allow my physical experience to impact on my performance, that is a choice I make. Given my choices are either to revert to a child-like state or allow some of the attention that should be given to the matters of the meeting to be diverted to managing my physical discomfort, my placement in the figured world is clear; I am unimportant and my comfort is not worth considering.

Trust/mistrust

Along with demonstrations of my lack of importance in the figured world is the positioning of myself, and other workers (who are not managers) as untrustworthy. As Smyth (2017, pp. 215, 211) argues:

> The managerialist paradigm starts from the unfounded presumption that academics cannot be trusted, and that academic work has to be 'managed', curbed, audited and generally distrusted ... all the visioning capacity resides in the superordinate positions (i.e. those 'officially' designated as the leaders), and those to be removed on the grounds of incompetence are the recalcitrant subordinates (the workers), who by definition of their not being 'leaders', are incapable of having visions.

Neoliberal managerialism is often claimed to look like a form of feudalism (Klikauer & Tabassum, 2019; Spicer, 2018) with the role of workers captured in the proverb: 'When the great lord passes the peasants bow deeply and silently fart' (<https://www.quora.com/What-is-the-meaning-of-the-proverb-%E2%80%98When-the-great-lord-passes-the-peasants-bow-deeply-and-silently-fart-%E2%80%99>). In feudal times peasants did not question the great lord, they offered visible signs of homage and, as suggested in the proverb, may well have engaged in surreptitious acts of defiance, but these acts of defiance had to remain hidden. In medieval times, peasants and serfs certainly did not trust that the great lords had their welfare at heart and any protection they received from the lord often arose from their own actions when they were coerced into his fighting forces with inadequate training, and minimal arms with which to protect themselves. Great lords employed staff whose sole responsibility was to ensure peasants paid rent for their land regularly, that the crops and stock they had were appropriately measured so that taxes and tithes were calculated correctly, and that the required free work for the church was undertaken appropriately. In 1395 Jean Froissart wrote:

> It is the custom in England, as with other countries, for the nobility to have great power over the common people, who are serfs. This means that they are bound by law and custom to plough the field of their masters, harvest the corn, gather it into barns, and thresh and winnow the grain; they must also mow and carry home the hay, cut and collect wood, and perform all manner of tasks of this kind. (<https://www. historylearningsite.co.uk/medieval-england/the-lifestyle-of-medieval-peasants/>)

Translating this to modern times, I argue that neoliberal managerialist ideology positions workers in a similar manner. They are employed to do particular forms of work, and management invest time and effort into ensuring that these tasks are not only performed, but performed the way management want them to be performed. 'Workers are disregarded, discarded, and ideologically reframed' (Klikauer & Tabassum, 2019, p. 88). This ideological reframing positions workers as untrustworthy, of less worth and their personhood is unimportant; they are only valuable as human capital, just as in medieval times, peasants and serfs were only valuable for what they produced through their labour. 'Management determine what shall transpire' (Smyth, 2017, p. 156) and workers provide appropriate fodder to be identified as scapegoats when things go wrong, and as problems successfully overcome when things go right.

In universities, management no longer trust workers to perform the work they are employed to do (Connell, 2019a) and therefore feel justified in creating ever more intrusive forms of supervision. This is increasingly being experienced by workers as micro-management and even bullying (Kirkby & Reiger, 2015; Sims, 2019a). 'The audit regime now entrenched in universities embeds, even flaunts, managers' distrust of the workforce' (Connell, 2019b, p. vi). Staff are expected to simply comply with managerial demands, and those who question are positioned as trouble-makers, people who do not have the wellbeing of the organisation at heart, and/or people who are simply old-fashioned, unrealistic and resistant to change (Kirkby & Reiger, 2015). In this figured world, staff are identified as problems, rather than as key resources needed to deliver the business of the organisation. This is particularly challenging in the higher education environment where traditionally academics, in particular, have been expected to engage in debate, to ask hard questions, to hold managers and themselves to account, and to work collegially with managers to govern the organisation (Bessant, 2015).

This lack of trust is reflected in increasing numbers of policies and procedures that govern what should be done, by whom and how. In the manifesto developed by staff at the University of Aberdeen (2016, p. 3), it is pointed out that: 'Loss of trust is the greatest enemy of academic freedom since it leads to the replacement of autonomy and self-determination with surveillance and control.' The problem with this lack of trust is that it becomes internalised as the appropriate way to behave in the figured world so that the 'deadening quality and self-serving circularity of managerial ethics seem to hint at a desire to climb back into the amniotic sack of memo and committee-inspired tranquillity' (Taylor, 2003, p. 20).

Procedures around taking annual leave are a good example of the imposition of tighter controls and the consequence loss of academic autonomy. In order to take leave I now have to indicate on the application form that all my duties are covered in my absence (this doesn't appear to apply equally across all sectors of the university as I have experienced delays in obtaining answers for certain queries many times because the person who needed to answer was on leave). On more than one occasion I have had to identify who was covering my teaching, even when I was taking leave in a trimester in which I was not teaching. At other times colleagues who had organised cover were still refused leave because the day or two sought were in their teaching trimester. Organizing cover takes time (even when it is cover for non-existent work), and those who undertake to cover do not get any official workload recognition; it is therefore volunteer work undertaken in order for colleagues to exercise their legal right to annual leave. Such requirements are imposed presumably because management do not trust staff to take leave in a responsible manner. Of course, monitoring leave, and doing the initial check that the application is correct before passing it on to a manager to approve requires time and resources, as does developing the relevant forms and policies. Managers therefore need a coterie of lower level administrative staff to do this checking work. In many organisations these staff simply experience an intensification of workload, as additional work is piled on to them, accompanied by an increase in managerial positions (what Graeber & Cerutti, 2018, call bullshit jobs) to oversee this work and to develop the relevant policies and procedures. Such policies and procedures cannot possibly be developed by those who understand the realities of the work they are governing, rather they have to be developed by managers who are as remote as possible from the actual work so that the policies can remain 'pure' rather than risk contamination from reality.

Lack of trust goes both ways. As the gap between managers and workers widens, workers are less and less likely to trust managers (Monbiot, 2017), particularly those who appear secure in their 'well-remunerated privilege and who are nonetheless busily engaged in merciless practices of "cutting" and "tightening"' (Kenway et al., 2015, p. 266). Following neoliberal managerial privilege, managers commonly pass on a range of work to subordinates arguing 'they were too busy to do such things themselves, leading, of course, to their having even less to do than previously' (Graeber, 2019, p. 33) resulting in work overload for subordinates. In many cases these subordinates end up doing the managers' jobs (without formal recognition of such), which frees managers to perform other important work, such as developing more intrusive monitoring systems, and developing more and more policies and procedures to 'improve' the organisation's performance.

What I see here is the privileging of the role of management in operating rather like a feudal lord. Management perspective is reified, workers are untrustworthy and must be intensively surveilled to ensure that they do the work for which they are paid. Multitudes of policies and procedures identify what should be done, how, and by whom. Neoliberal managerial bullshit discourse positions this as natural; this is the way of the world and we should all accept our allocated status and roles.

Democracy/autocracy

As discussed above, inequality is a goal of neoliberalism. In this sense, 'liberty depends on preventing the majority from exercising choice over the direction that politics and society might take' (Monbiot, 2017, p. 32). The elite should be the decision-makers; they have the 'right' information and the 'right' values. In contrast, 'the public are ignorant and meddlesome outsiders. They have to be put in their place ... The "herd" must remain "bewildered"' (Chomsky, 2013a, pp. 4, 5). Democratic governance should be replaced by governance of the elite (Smyth, 2017). Illustrating this in his reactionary manifesto, Anissimov (2013) argued that democracy is fatally flawed, and it is better to discard it completely, that people can never be equal and we should stop expecting this, and that the political right is right, and left is wrong.

The classic definition of democracy [as defined by the Merriam-Webster dictionary: 'a government in which the supreme power is vested in the people and exercised by them directly or indirectly through a system of representation usually involving periodically held free elections' (<https://www.merriam-webster.com/dictionary/democracy>) is not what we see in modern democracies. Politically, wealth defines political voice. In America Chomsky (2013a) argues that 70 per cent of the population are disenfranchised, and that about a tenth of the richest 1 per cent of the population have the power to ensure legislation and policies are developed that get them what they want. Billionaires behave in increasingly fascist ways, using their power to capture more of the market and to coerce others into consuming their services and products to increase their monopoly (Means & Slater, 2019). Under neoliberal ideology this is not problematic; rather the majority of the population are expected to exercise their 'voice' (their power) through spending, not through participating in decision-making. Unfortunately, as Monbiot (2016) points out, not everyone has the same spending power so even in the world of consumption, there are those whose 'voices' are not heard; disenfranchisement thus tends to focus around those on lower (and even middle) incomes.

This scenario is played out in organisations through differential access to power for managers compared to workers. The privilege associated with management creates a situation in which management perspectives are valued more highly than are the ideas of workers. Over 10 years ago (Saunders, 2006, p. 15) wrote 'a cowed and compliant academic workforce' are identified as important for 'a university's economic health.' In other words, successful organisations are not positioned as operating on democratic principles. Vivek Wadhwa, Director of Research, Duke University's Centre for Entrepreneurship and Research Commercialization, argues that the best leadership model operating in the best companies in the world is that of enlightened dictatorship (Wadhwa, 2016). 'People love to follow strong leaders' (p. 2), he states.

Workplaces, under neoliberal managerialism, have become dictatorships (E. Anderson, 2019, p. 63) where privileged management 'impose controls on workers that are unconstitutional for democratic states to impose on citizens.' Whilst in Australia there are some protections in industrial law, and in enterprise agreements, increasingly managements are attempting to dismantle these. For example, in the most recent Australian university bargaining round, university managements of various universities across the country increasingly attacked transparent controls on workloads in enterprise agreements, arguing that such controls are better located in policy (where they can be changed at management whim) rather than in agreements (where they are legally enforceable). Some employers are now checking employees' Facebook pages and their activity on social media. Anderson tells of companies in America (where health cover comes from employers) that are requiring staff to engage in particular health practices with an impost on their salaries should they not do so.

Moves towards totalitarianism in the workplace are accompanied by bullshit claims around staff consultation and staff participation in decision-making and governance. I identify these as bullshit claims because, whilst they are couched in terms of opportunities for staff to provide input into decisions, in reality they have no substance. In my experiences, consultation means me spending time putting together a written submission on a particular issue (usually at a moment's notice, with minimal time before submissions close). What I have shared in my feedback appears to dive into a black hole once submitted, never to be seen or heard from thereafter. There is rarely any evidence that anything I, or my colleagues, have provided as feedback has even been read, let alone considered in the final decision. Occasionally we are invited to a meeting where management offer to share something of importance (to them) with staff with opportunities for us to ask questions and provide feedback. Invariably what this means is that management (sometimes one person, other times a cast of two or three) speak to the audience for at least 50 minutes (accompanied by power-point and filmed so the presentation can go online for those lucky people who managed to miss the session). At the end of the presentation questions from the audience are sought. Rarely are any such questions answered in any other way except with meaningless bullshit, and the session is quickly drawn to a close after a couple of questions and non-answers. My experiences are not unique. Over 15 years ago Taylor (2003, p. 16) wrote: 'Managerialism rests upon a circularity of information and information-producing systems all too apparent to academics who instinctively already know the eventual results of a "consultative process" when it is first announced.' Despite protests to the contrary, my experience leads me to believe that decisions are made in advance of 'consultations' so that consultative processes are simply steps that need to be shown to be performed (perhaps to demonstrate to gullible staff that things are being done properly), generating information that is only used if it supports the already-made decision.

I might argue that the only meaningful consultation in which I have had an opportunity to participate in recent years is the Voice Survey. At UNE this is run every few years (in 2019 by the Voice Project <https:// www.voiceproject.com/>). Despite its claims to be anonymous, the last page of the survey in 2019 asked for demographic data: age, location, time at UNE for example. Given I am the one and only female professor in the School of Education any anonymity is a pipedream, and whilst I was willing to stand by all I wrote in that survey, I know of a number of people who did not complete it because once they arrived on the final page they were afraid that filling in the required information would lead to identification. A number chose to exit at that point, presumably losing the feedback they had provided, whilst others claimed they had made up an identity as different as possible from who they really were. Thus, the climate of fear that pervades much of my workplace significantly limited the number of respondents and may well have limited the usefulness of the survey results as a consequence. Certainly, the people who spoke to me about the survey were people who had significant comments to make about elements of the university's functioning that they did not feel safe to share via this survey.

Taking a slightly different perspective, West (2016) argues that consultations are set up, not to gather the perspectives of staff, but as opportunities for staff to demonstrate their loyalty to management; in other words for potential managers to identify their willingness to follow management script in the hope that their demonstrated compliance will be rewarded with a promotion. 'Dissenters are casually dismissed as poor team-players, trouble-makers or malcontents' (p. 6) so their perspectives can be dismissed without consideration. In contrast:

> the modern university most rewards those who demonstrate both loyalty to superiors and effective control of subordinates. Good managers are those who gets things done, which tends to mean that they are not hampered by either sensitivity for others' feelings or democratic scruples. (p. 6)

The reality of these experiences clashes with the ways in which universities have been operating for centuries, and certainly with the ways in which universities operated in my early career experiences. Whilst not claiming the past is a lost utopia, universities were once democratic in their operations; they were characterized by considerable staff involvement in governance, in particular through Academic Boards and University Councils/Senates (I will use the term Council as this is what this governance group is called in my most recent experience, but acknowledge that this is not the term used universally around Australia), but also through groups of staff such as the professoriate. However, more recent thinking, aligning with neoliberalism, positions staff involvement in governance in a much more negative light: for example, according to P. Adams (2019, p. 28) the 2016 Price Waterhouse Coopers and Australian Higher Education Industrial Association (2016) report argued: 'academic freedom and democratic governance of Universities interfere with the efficient exercise of managerial prerogative and must be reduced in influence.'

This positioning is reflected in what we now see in the erosion of a democratic approach to governance (Brennan & Zipin, 2019; J. Ross,

2019b; Shattock, 2019) which, as a consequence, and contrary to neo-liberal ideology, poses significant risks to the organisation. Spicer (2018) argues that professional knowledge (of the organisation, of the product being sold, or in the case of universities, of education itself) is essential to ensure that decision-making is realistic. In the failure of the Nokia company, he argued that 'large mismatches between the image created by bullshit and the underlying reality were overlooked' (p.141). Mismatches are more likely the more remote members of governance are from the organisation. In the case of universities, the majority of those on Councils now tend to be business people, most of whom at some point attended university as a student, but whose current contact with universities, and understanding of the higher education sector, are extremely limited and who therefore find it easy to impose neoliberal managerial thinking. Around Australia over half the Chancellors now have a business background, compared to around a third 10 years ago. Elected staff representatives have declined from around 17 per cent to 14 per cent (J. Ross, 2019b). In my own experience, over my time on Council, staff representation was decreased from two elected academic staff representatives to one, and student representation was also decreased from two to one. At the same time, Academic Boards, who in the past had supreme authority in academic matters (Shattock, 2019), are now increasingly subject to Council approval. A similar situation is evident in the UK:

> In some universities lay members are seeking access to senates and academic boards to assure themselves as to the processes of academic decision-making. This has the potential to be the thin end of the wedge of lay intrusion into what is taught and by whom. (Shattock, 2019, p. 6)

In their recent manifesto, the Australian Association of University Professors (2019, p. 3) argued that by 2030 they hoped that this ground could be re-captured and that:

5. Universities should be led by a distinguished and respected scholar who regularly consults with the professoriate on the running of the university
6. Academics should be effectively engaged in university governance, with the professoriate providing leadership of disciplines, acting as mentors, and promoting academic values.

Whilst this might be a dream for universities, we are operating in a context that is no longer a democracy. Neoliberalism and managerialism have combined to create an overarching ideology that drives a system where:

> it is of extreme importance that we become the stupid nation, not misled by science and rationality, in the interests of the short-term gains of the masters of the economy and political system, and damn the consequences. (Chomsky, 2013b, pp. 3–4)

In other words, the privileging of management is an attack on democracy made invisible through the bullshit discourse that justifies it on the basis of quality decision-making and efficiency.

Lack of status of workers performing core work

One of the casualties of this neoliberal managerial drive to disempower staff is the concept of secure employment. The number of casuals employed in Australian higher education has more than doubled across the years 1990 to 2005 (Klopper & Power, 2014). At some universities nearly 80 per cent of undergraduate teaching is performed by casual academics (Wardale, Richardson, & Suseno, 2019). An analysis of the WGEA data (2017–2018) compiled by Richard Bailey and provided to NTEU organisers indicates that rates of casualisation ranged from 32.11 per cent casual and 43.41 per cent insecure at Notre Dame to 56.10 per cent casual and 74.97 per cent insecure at the University of Tasmania. Thus, rates of permanency ranged from 25.03 per cent to 56.59 per cent. Across the Australian higher education sector in mid-2018 approximately 94,500 people were employed as casuals. Wardale et al. (2019) claim that the Australian higher education sector is the third largest employer of casuals nationally. It is not uncommon for casuals to have had a series of contracts for a longer period than ongoing employees have been with a particular employer.

In the figured world of Australian higher education staff are simply viewed as human capital (Taberner, 2018) and the role of managers is to 'extract the maximum out of each employee while, at the same time, rewarding them for their efforts at the lowest possible wage' (p. 135). Casual work is particularly attractive to managers because it is much less expensive: staff are only paid for specific tasks and the time allocated to doing each of these tasks is systematically reduced so that most casual academics with whom I work 'volunteer' many more hours than those for which they are paid. Watts (2017, p. 337) argues that this increasing casualisation in the work of teaching is a deliberate strategy aimed at reducing the cost of teaching (the core work of the university) to enable funds to be diverted into other areas such as research, and 'corporate pay scales for senior managers.'

Casualisation is most often 'camouflaged' using bullshit discourse, 'as being part of strategic management and being flexible' (Klikauer & Tabassum, 2019, p. 90). Labour that is perceived as available on call, but easily disposed of when not required is what is sometimes called gig labour (Means & Slater, 2019). Whilst employer groups often identify the flexibility associated with the gig economy as something workers want (Education and Policy Team, 2016), flexibility has become a bullshit term that is used to obscure the reality of casualisation. This reality includes a lack of protection for basic employment rights (such as sick leave, holidays) as well as limited access to superannuation, health care and the pressure of expectations for work beyond that for which they are paid (Wood, Graham, Lehdonvirta, & Hjorth, 2019). Casuals are not entitled to automatic pay increments and, in a recent case in which I was involved in the Fair Work Commission [National Tertiary Education Industry Union-NSW Division v The University of New England T/A The University of New England (C2018/1250)], they can have their hourly rate cut by two thirds with no warning and no diminution of responsibilities. Thus this flexibility comes at significant cost to casual employees who experience a kind of 'fictitious freedom' whilst being locked into low skilled, low paid, lowly valued and often fragmented tasks (Shibata, 2019) that do not enhance their chances of permanent employment.

This 'flexibility' also comes at a cost to the core business of the university: that of delivering quality teaching (Percy & Beaumont, 2008). Poorly resourced, poorly supported and poorly paid casual academics struggle to preserve quality in the face of almost impossible expectations. In my experience, the work needed to update content in units each time they are taught is expected as part of the work associated with unit co-ordination, but this work is not paid. As a consequence, it is only fair to expect casual academics to undertake minor tweaking (such as changing a couple of instructions in an assignment briefing, amending assignment due dates, and maybe providing an additional new reading). Major work such as reorganizing unit content to match a new textbook, introducing whole new topics, or amending to match a national curriculum change are not reasonable expectations to hold. Thus, in a time of chronic short-staffing, in my experience there are units in courses that are taught year after year with only minor modifications because they are consistently staffed by casual academics.

There is another cost to increasing casualisation. 'Precarity has become a new form of regulation of the educational worker and it creates new subjectivities that are expected to confirm to market norms' (Blackmore, 2019a, p. 182). Blackmore is referring to the imbalance of power in the employment relationship that arises when casual academics are dependent on the good will of management for each successive short-term contract. Academics in this position are not able to speak openly or be heard to criticize management nor the institution in any way.

> Although an administrator may be prohibited by university policy from dismissing an instructor because that administrator disagrees with the ideas the instructor is presenting in class or with that faculty member's scholarship, in the absence of stringent enforced regulations it does not require much acumen to simply remove that employee from the next round of course assignments without giving any reason other than 'scheduling changes'. (Murray, 2019, p. 240)

Thus, although limits to academic freedom are not identified as problematic in Australia (French, 2019), the increasing casualisation of the workforce results in considerable restrictions that are hidden from view because casuals are not considered part of the academic workforce.

There are other negative impacts of increasing casualisation; impacts related to social justice and the current trends around the world towards privileging of white masculinities. O'Keefe and Courtois (2019) suggest that women casuals tend to be assigned 'the housework' of the academy: work that is time consuming but not of the sort that will place them on the path towards permanent employment. In their study women were more likely to be on hourly rate contracts or zero-hour contracts whereas men in casual academic employment were more likely to have year-long or multiple-year contracts. The women on average had spent longer in precarious employment (7.1 years) than the men (5.7 years). One participant in the research had been in temporary positions for 18 years and another was still being employed hourly after 13 years. I have worked with casual academics who have been employed casually for over 20 years. As a consequence, women working casually in higher education 'experience poverty, insecurity and economic dependence. Many academic women are in effect part of the working poor' (O'Keefe & Courtois, 2019, p. 473).

Gender is not the only basis on which discrimination against casual employees may manifest (Murray, 2019). In our current neoliberal neo-conservative world, more and more people are tending towards right wing privileging of white masculinity and a disdain for those who do not fit their conception of 'the norm'. 'These shared objects of loathing, to neo-conservative eyes, represent the decline of masculinist western civilisation and its colonisation by undesirable Others (immigrants, the undeserving poor, ethnic minorities, "liberated" women, LGBTIQ people)' (Gray & Nicholas, 2019, p. 272). For example, I am aware of complaints laid by students who claim they cannot understand the speech of academics for whom English is not the first language. In the cases I have witnessed, the academics had all received their doctorates from English-speaking universities and, whilst they spoke with an accent, I found neither their writing nor their speech incomprehensible. However, had those academics been casually employed, it would have been tempting for management to avoid future student complaints (and the work associated in dealing with these) by simply not offering them further work. Given the 'higher education landscape is characterised by institutional and everyday sexism, racism, homophobia and ableism, then it is not a safe space to work for those existing outside of normative paradigms' (Gray & Nicholas, 2019, p. 276), and it is not a space where casual academics existing outside normative paradigms can make a living.

Summary

In the figured world of my university (and many others I am told) the privilege associated with management is largely unrecognised because it is obscured by a bullshit discourse arising from neoliberal managerialism. This bullshit discourse positions decision-making by management as the most efficient way of doing things: management have the skills, knowledge and overview that workers lack therefore they are in the best position to make decisions. Staff are placated by pseudo-consultations and fake opportunities to provide feedback. When there is no evidence that any input has been considered, staff have been sufficiently 'educated' to perceive this as managers having more information than themselves, therefore decisions must have taken other things onto consideration about which they know nothing. Just like feudal peasants, workers shrug and get on with what they are doing.

At the same time management increasingly divorce themselves from the day-to-day reality of the core work of the university (I remember in one Council meeting being asked to show Council members one of my online Moodle sites, to the accompaniment of comments such as 'I have never seen our online sites before' from not only Council members but senior management). Creating a gap between management and staff contributes to the mystique that surrounds management decision-making: staff cannot see what management do all day and therefore are expected to trust that really important work is being done without ever seeing any evidence of the impact of that work on their day-to-day realities (unless it is to subject them to another meaningless process, audit, form to complete or request for information needed by yesterday).

Privileging of management is accompanied by the concomitant devaluation of not only workers, but of the work they do, the core work of the university. This is particularly evident in the devaluing of online teaching. There is one school of thought, promulgated at UNE by a previous Vice Chancellor, that online teaching should be done as cheaply as possible (following the MOOC model), with content pre-loaded and students interacting with each other, supported by a para-professional who can be paid on a considerably lower scale than an academic. This model aims to free enough funding to create a small on-campus cohort of those with sufficient privilege to afford to join the elite group. That such a view has not substantially changed is evidenced by the case in the Fair Work Commission to which I referred above (where casual academics teaching online had their pay cut by two thirds based on the argument that interacting with individual students asynchronously rather than having a group tutorial is not teaching). The lack of value of management for the core work of the university is also evidenced by the chronic under-staffing in academic teams, whist simultaneously recruiting in a substantial number of management positions. When management need help to operate increasingly onerous compliance processes it seems that help is quickly forthcoming. When academic teams need help to teach students, that help is delayed significantly (to the tune of two years and still counting in some cases).

Managerial privilege places modern managers in positions similar to that of feudal lords. Organisations operate with systems of controls that are undemocratic, inequitable and unjust. Workers are placed in subordinate positions where their every move is increasingly scrutinized by increasingly onerous reporting regimes. However, in neoliberal managerial parlance this is justified on the grounds that such an approach generates quality. Bullshit discourse focuses on the need to be accountable. No one would argue that we should not be accountable for the government funds spent, however accountability does not need to be accompanied by an assumption that workers cannot be trusted to do the work for which they are employed. Particularly in the case of universities, workers are more likely to perceive their work as a vocation; increasing audit requirements, rather than increasing efficiency, actually hamper productivity. Management remain oblivious to this as they operate within a rarefied figured world of their own privilege that blinds them to the realities of those whom they are managing.

CHAPTER 5

The figured world of managers/leaders

I sat in an office around a table with a colleague, our NTEU Industrial Officer and two managers. We were discussing the steps management had devised for a Change Management process for a directorate which employed professional staff. As my colleagues and myself read our Enterprise Agreement the process required:

1. *A matching of existing positions to new positions based on Position Descriptions;*
2. *A transfer into the new positions if there is a direct match;*
3. *Where there is no direct match staff are placed on a redeployment register where they are given employment for a particular duration, given first priority in any positions that come available, and have the choice of taking a redundancy; and*
4. *Where a staff member is successfully redeployed there is a requirement that, should the salary and/or grade of the new position be lower than in the previous position, the previous salary and/or grade is maintained until such times as annual increments in the new position 'catch up' (a salary maintenance provision).*

However, in this particular case, management had inserted another step between not being matched and being placed on the redeployment register. Where there were jobs available in the new directorate (only this directorate, not other places in the university) not filled by the matching process, those who were not matched were offered the opportunity to apply through a simple 'Expression of Interest' process. However, in choosing to do so, the employee was required to accept the salary and conditions that applied to the new position. This means that in choosing to lodge an EOI, an employee could be in the position of having to accept a lower salary and grade than had been held prior to the Change Management process. Management argued that the salary maintenance clause in the Agreement did not apply until the employee was placed on the Redeployment List. They argued that their EOI step came before this happened. In other words, redeployment and salary maintenance happened when the change management process was complete, and it was not complete, they claimed, until AFTER the EOI process.

We were aware that employees were in something of a cleft stick. Anyone unmatched could refuse to put in an EOI for the remaining unmatched positions in their Directorate, but there were less positions than there were unmatched staff, so not putting in an EOI ran the risk of missing out on a job in the current Directorate. That meant being put on the redeployment list and hoping that a position came up in the next few months somewhere else in the university. However, putting in an EOI for the remaining unmatched positions meant for some a decrease in salary and grade. As union representatives we wanted to prevent this and so notified a dispute.

In the preliminary meeting to this dispute management were very clear. As far as they were concerned they were offering unmatched staff a choice. They argued that it was better for staff to clear away the uncertainty and stress of workplace change as quickly as possible by offering unmatched staff this quick and easy option of getting a secure position. I don't think I'll ever forget the look of bafflement on one manager's face when I argued (with considerable vigour!) that this is not a fair choice; that s/he was asking staff to choose between a rock and a hard place. 'But it's their choice,' was said again and again with varying degrees of emphasis. Phrases like: 'we want to make it easy for staff,' and 'we recognise this is a stressful time and we want to get staff into secure positions as quickly as we can,' were parroted at frequent intervals. Those sitting on the management side of the table seemed to genuinely believe that this additional step (that reduced salary and grade for more than one staff member) was something good that they were doing for staff. It appeared completely beyond their understanding that this was not a good choice to offer staff, and in fact, was something that we saw as oppressive and unfair. Whilst being harangued again about how wonderful management were for offering this new choice, I wondered how many in management would happily take a cut in pay and a lower status position, and how they thought it was a good thing for staff already paid at a low level.

When thinking about this incident in writing this chapter I reflected on how management, and those in higher status positions appeared to have no conception of reality. This was vividly illustrated to me by the recent whinge from our local federal MP, Barnaby Joyce. The headlines say it all: 'Poor Baby Barnaby Joyce says he's "struggling" on a $211,000 salary' (Langford, 2019). One of the respondents to this article, Jim Pembroke, pointed out that at the very point in time Joyce was heard to complain, the median wage was $65,000, the minimum wage $38,000 and those receiving Newstart (the unemployment benefit for those seeking work) got $14,500. The reality for those in elite groups appears to be very different from the reality for less fortunate members of society.

It seems to me that in the figured world of higher education (and even in society itself) the gap between those who are privileged and those who are not is huge, so significant, in fact, that there appears to be no understanding of the realities of life for those in a group other than one's own. In organisations, management have divorced themselves from workers and occupy their own figured world. As I discussed in the previous chapter, the figured world of management is one of privilege, often unrecognised and invisible, but privilege all the same. This element is illustrated as the dark grey box in Figure 4. The biggest outward sign of that privilege is evident in salaries.

Salary and title define worth

The focus on market forces in neoliberalism is used to justify extremely large (and ever increasing) managerial salaries, a form of corporate greed (Hil, 2012). Increasing inequality is a cornerstone of neoliberalism as it represents the 'strategy of the capitalist classes in alliance especially with financial managers to strengthen their hegemony and to expand the reach of financial markets' leading to 'levels of inequality last seen in the late nineteenth century' (Watts, 2017, p. 113). This inequity is reinforced through cost cutting on workers in order to free sufficient funds to pay

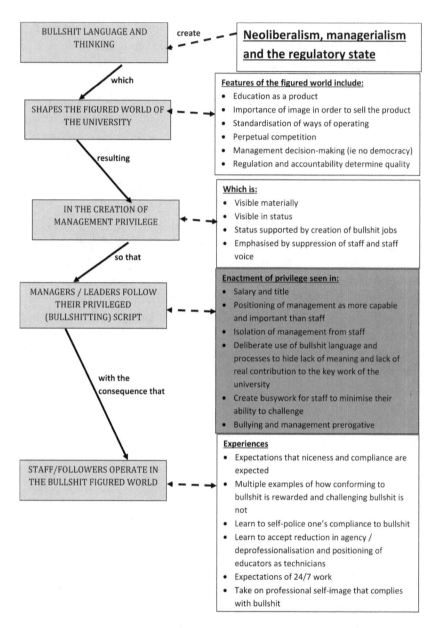

Figure 4. The enactment of privilege in the conceptual framework

inflated salaries to management 'further concentrating wealth and enhancing the power of capital over labor' (Means & Slater, 2019, p. 167).

The higher education sector is no different in this respect than the corporate sector. Even the title of Vice Chancellor is now expanded in order to align the position more clearly in the bullshit language of business: for example, it is not uncommon to see the title 'Vice Chancellor and CEO' or 'Vice Chancellor and President'. This label clearly differentiates the role of the nominal head of the organisation as something different from the academic colleague role that once encompassed Vice Chancellor duties.

The outcry over the salary of the Vice Chancellor's salary at the University of Bath in the UK in 2017/18, the highest paid Vice Chancellor in the UK at the time (R. Adams, 2017), drew attention to the growing disparity between the salaries of senior management in higher education and those of workers. This inequity is not evident only in the UK. Lyons and Hill (2018) report that the Australian Vice Chancellors with the highest salaries earn at least 1.5 times more than the then Vice Chancellor of Bath, and that the Bath salary at the time only ranked 28th out of the 38 Vice Chancellors in Australia. In 2017, of the 38 Australian public university Vice Chancellors, 13 were earning over a million dollars a year (J. Ross, 2019b), and by 2018 that number had risen to 16, with the average being A\$982,900 (J. Ross, 2019d). In many cases, casual academics take more than a year to earn what Vice Chancellors take home each week (Lyons & Hill, 2018). The highest paid Vice Chancellor in Australia in 2017 was the retiring Vice Chancellor of Melbourne University who was paid \$1.59 million (J. Ross, 2019a). The Vice Chancellor of Sydney University received a 56 per cent pay increase over a period of his five-year appointment to 2016, ending with a salary of \$1.4 million (Lyons & Hill, 2018) at a time when the national minimum wage increase between 2012 and 2016 was around 9.8 per cent. On average, Australian Vice Chancellors received a 5.1 per cent pay increase in 2018 at a time when the national worker pay increase was, on average, 2.3 per cent (J. Ross, 2019d). In the UK, Vice Chancellors, on average, earned around 6.4 times more than their workers and nearly half of them were members of the committee that set their salaries (Rudgard, 2018).

This difference in salary is justified in the language of neoliberal managerialism given that inequality is positioned as virtuous, the reward for one's position in the elite group (Monbiot, 2016); basically because 'some individuals are just better than others and deserve more' (Cody, 2019, p. 11).

However, in contrast to the bullshit, it appears that managerial salaries do not reflect actual performance (Cooper, Gulen, & Rau, 2016; Fitza, 2017; Hymas, 2018; Matousek & Tzeremes, 2016; Rhodes & Fleming, 2018). A study of 429 large US companies demonstrated that between 2006 and 2015, CEOs of companies who received the largest equity incentives performed significantly worse than companies where CEOs were paid less (Marshall & Lee, 2016). In the UK, Johnes and Virmani (2019) examined Vice Chancellor salaries in the period 2009–2017 looking at managerial efficiency, performance in university rankings and the financial status of the university and found that 'the main measure of performance which affects VC pay is the one based on media rankings' (p. 1). There appears to be little evidence that increases in pay result in performance improvements (Gschwandtner & McManus, 2018). To the contrary, the Gschwandtner and McManus study suggested that pay increases arose more from a keeping-up-with-the-Joneses approach given that universities paying their Vice Chancellors less were more likely to offer greater pay increases with little or no evidence of performance improvements. Graeber (2019) argues that efficiency is less and less required from managers the higher they climb in the hierarchy (certainly in my experience managers are not as accountable for their decisions as are teaching and research staff) meaning that the bullshit positioning of these high salaries as the reward for excellence in performance is just that: bullshit.

Whilst neoliberalism and managerialism together create a figured world where human capital theory justifies high salaries for labour performed by the elite (management), the expectation is that these salaries will continue to be offered to ensure that management positions remain competitive with those in the corporate sector. Unfortunately, this 'corporate fiction is a very different entity from the conception of the university as a community of scholars – academics and their students – united, as it were, in dispute over different philosophies, beliefs and practices' (Hayes, 2019,

p. 2). In taking on this corporate fiction (a bullshit discourse) managers are now prioritizing money over the pursuit of truth (Saunders, 2006). In the neoliberal managerial bullshit lexicon, only that which is 'monetised is valued' (Blackmore, 2019a, p. 183), and thus, by definition, managers must be valued much more highly than workers, must be more trustworthy than workers, and therefore their excessive remuneration must not only be valid but must be stringently defended to maintain appropriate differentiation between the trusted and the non-trusted; between the valued and the de-valued human capital used to generate the income necessary to pay these inflated salaries.

Once membership in this world of privilege is established, be-longing is cemented by the awarding (or usurpation) of academic titles. In Australian higher education, academics follow an upwards career path from Associate Lecturer, through to Lecturer, Senior Lecturer, Associate Professor and Professor. Progression is through a promotion application which requires demonstration of achievements at the higher level over a sustained period of time. Many academics in Australia find it easier to apply for a position at the next level at another university than they do to progress their careers through internal promotion applications. Achieving the title 'Professor' is recognition of world-class achievement in academia and demonstration of many years' worth of high-level (national and inter-national) performance. The draft UNE Academic Profiles, for example, position a Level E position (i.e. a professor) as someone who has dem-onstrated 'outstanding performance and pre-eminence as a scholar of international standing.' This includes a distinguished profile in teaching, supervision and research leadership, as well as distinguished contribution to service and engagement. In other words, in Australian academia, the title 'Professor' is one that is awarded on the basis of distinguished aca-demic performance. However, it is increasingly common for managers appointed into a range of management positions to be given the title of 'Professor.' This title goes with the management role and does not reflect any form of academic achievement that may, or may not, be possessed the particular manager appointed. This usurpation of the academic title makes me feel as if my own achievements in gaining the title through my academic performance are somehow debased.

Management style

In my experience there is little leadership evidenced by managers, rather their role is a managerial one where management has become positioned as the most important purpose of the university (in ways similar to those discussed by Morrish, 2016). Smyth (2017, p. 156) supports this claim, arguing: 'academics are being given an unambiguous lesson that they are subservient to the "clerks" in the university – it is "management" that determines what shall transpire.'

It is not uncommon to find middle management positions filled by those who previously worked as academics. Whilst their previous colleagues might expect these managers to be more understanding of the realities of their figured world, these managers tend to be quickly encultured into the figured world of management, leaving their ex-colleagues to feel betrayed (Barcan, 2019). It seems these managers find the way to survive the transition is to be 'willing to abandon values their own education might have instilled in them and adopt those of the government, public service and university hierarchs they now serve' (Saunders, 2006, p. 10). Hil (2012, p. 182) called these managers 'para-academics' and claimed in general they:

> do little or no research, and devote themselves with feverish intensity to form-filling, co-ordination duties and committee-attendance. They are characterised by an uncompromising devotion to administrative activities, irrespective of the pain inflicted upon themselves and others by stressful work regimes. For the para-academic, adherence to authority is the name of the game.

In contrast, appointing managers from outside the ranks of academia is becoming increasingly common, and the norm in higher levels of management. This strategy is based on the assumption that management is a stand-alone skill set and domain-specific knowledge is not needed, and may in fact be a hindrance (Zheng, Graham, Epitropaki, & Snape, 2019). This is nowhere more evident than in the appointment of chancellors with a corporate rather than an academic background. Around 3 per cent of Australia's chancellors are career academics compared to 53 per cent from a corporate background (J. Ross, 2019a).

These trends mean that managers are well inculcated into the ideologies of neoliberal managerialism as they perform their roles. How they go about this role performance depends to some extent on the kind of personality traits, values, knowledge and skills they bring into the management arena. Firstly, there is an association between neoliberal thinking and right-wing authoritarianism and social dominance (Azevedo & Jost, 2019). Further, right wing, authoritarian beliefs are associated with a low emotional IQ (Van Hiel et al., 2019). Those holding beliefs on the right are 'more likely to value tradition, social order, authority, conformity, hierarchy, and social stability' (Azevedo & Jost, 2019, p. 52); values managers can not only espouse but prioritize in their managerial roles.

In addition to this, there is a range of research in psychology examining the psychological impact of inequality in those who position themselves as superior. Beattie (2019, p. 102) claims the 'possession of power inhibits the ability to adopt the perspective of others or understand how they see the world, intuit the emotions of others or take into account their knowledge.' This self-centredness tends to result in increased levels of self-interest and narcissism and a commitment to competing with others in order to maintain status (Bettache & Chiu, 2019). There is also an increased tendency to blame-the-victim thinking and a positioning of relationships as only useful if they are self-serving (Beattie, Bettache, & Ching Yee Chong, 2019). These leadership traits have been characterized by McKoy (2013, p. 200) who used the term PICO which stands for 'power, influence, control, and over the top feelings of importance resembling a unique form of narcissism.' Increased wealth is found to be associated with a form of moral reasoning closely aligned to that identified in psychopaths, and there is a range of research suggesting that psychopathic personality disorder is more often found in today's business leaders than in a matched sample of committed psychiatric patients (Beattie, 2019). Moral reasoning tends to be limited to making decisions based on gain with much less emphasis on social concern. This notion that neoliberal managerial thinking impairs moral development is supported by a study of members of the US Congress. Ruske (2015) found that a degree in economics made it more likely a congress man/woman would behave corruptly compared to those in Congress who had other qualifications.

The characteristics managers bring with them into their roles interact with the expectations of them created in their figured world to shape their management style. In the figured world of higher education, leadership is most often enacted through various forms of authoritarianism leading into what Oplatka (2016) calls dark leadership. Dark leadership is characterized by the very traits that are discussed above: egocentric narcissism, emotional blindness and self-centred decision-making (Braun, Kark, & Wisse, 2019b). In the educational context, Oplatka added another two values: a limited view of education and a devaluing of the student-teacher relationship. D. Ross, Sasso, Matteson, and Matteson (2020) identify dark leadership as consisting of the dark triad of Machiavellianism, subclinical narcissism, and subclinical psychopathy. Dark leadership focuses on maintaining the illusion of control using strategies that (often unintentionally) harm both other people and the organisation in the longer term and may take several different forms depending on the extent to which harm is intended versus a consequence of incompetence (Milosevic, Maric, & Loncar, 2019). Destructive leaders are exploitative and quite ruthless although these characteristics are often hidden under a layer of charm that serves to recruit followers. I remember one colleague who was honestly bamboozled by our discussions in the staff room about the unfairness and bullying delivered by one particular manager until that colleague actually experienced some of this behaviour him/herself.

In contrast, abusive leaders engage in less overt charm and more overt signs of hostility that appear aimed at enhancing the leader's advantage or simply demonstrating the leaders' complete indifference towards others. Ineffective leaders are much less engaged in their leadership role and thus harm both their subordinates and the organisation through what they do not do. These leaders rarely bestir themselves to support their subordinates. Toxic leaders interfere with their subordinates' ability to work, often in an attempt to position themselves to an advantage, and thus tend to flourish in systems characterized by the kinds of proceduralism as described by Blackmore (2019b).

Taking a different perspective Braun, Kark, and Wisse (2019a) refer to what they call the three nightmare traits of dark leaders: dishonesty, disagreeableness and carelessness that link to reduced levels of honesty and humility. These nightmare traits align with those identified in the dark leadership literature as they emphasize the exploitative nature of leaders' interactions, including the element of dishonesty, the fundamental under-pinning of bullshit language. In her tongue-in-cheek paper, Dumitrescu (2019) offers 10 strategies to use upwards toxicity to improve one's own position in relation to others, all of which involve using nightmare traits to advantage oneself and disadvantage others. In my experience leaders working on the dark side have agreed to undertake actions they did not carry out (and maybe never intended to carry out); they have promised one thing but done something quite different, or even nothing at all. They have provided unclear and contradictory information about what needs to be done, perhaps to conceal their own lack of understanding of what needs to be done. They have refused staff benefits that they themselves enjoyed as academics; (for example reducing study leave from six to three months despite entitlement to six months and having taken six months themselves), and have refused to make decisions at all (referring the issue up the chain to others so that they hold no responsibility). These leader-ship characteristics shape the figured world in a range of ways and one of these key impacts is bullying.

Bullying

Safe Work Australia (2019) identify bullying as one of the potential haz-ards in the workplace managers are expected to address. It is somewhat ironic that, despite this legal responsibility, a number of researchers link bullying to managerial culture itself (Mayo, 2019; Sims, 2019a; Taberner, 2018; Watts, 2017), thereby calling onto doubt the efficacy of manage-ment strategies in reducing it. In higher education bullying is not only widespread (West, 2016; Young, 2017), but management does not 'simply foster bullying, it *is* bullying' (Saunders, 2006, p. 16: emphasis from the original). The expectations placed on managers to demonstrate their be-longing in their figured world are such that, if they were not bullies before their appointment, they soon learn to be so. As a consequence, around 80 per cent of bullying in higher education is perpetrated by managers (D. Ross et al., 2020). Sometimes this is accompanied by direct threats. For example, I recall an occasion where every staff member in my faculty received an email from a manager that was both a warning about the need to act professionally and an implied threat. While at the time, nobody whom I spoke to had the faintest idea what it was about, anecdotally I was much later told the incident that sparked the email involved two to three staff at the most. The email started with a story about a media article about a CEO who got into legal strife because of an incident of unprofessional behaviour when talking about colleagues. The email then went on to report the occurrence of supposedly similar behaviour involving a feud between staff and claimed that they had drawn students into the feud. In summing up, the manager then said she/he could and would, without hesitation, use the options available which included suspension of the offending staff member. Reading the email was unsettling because neither myself, nor the colleagues with whom I spoke, had any idea what it was about but we were clear we had been warned and threatened over behaviour in which we had not engaged. Whilst we were being told to act professionally, the email was clearly a very unprofessional way to deal with an isolated matter involving very few staff. The issue of staff bullying involving a few staff was dealt with by bullying a whole faculty.

In an international review, Keashly (2019) estimated that between a fifth and a half of staff in higher education have been bullied at least once a week over a 12-month period, and slightly higher numbers of staff have witnessed bullying. At least half of those bullied claim the bullying had persisted for at least three years, with around 10 per cent reporting bullying that lasted over five years. Keashly suggests that, given the prevalence and duration of bullying, only a minority of staff in higher education would have no exposure to bullying. Nearly half of the researchers in a UK survey of higher education claimed they had been direct targets of bullying or harassment, 61 per cent claimed they had witnessed bullying and/or harassment, and 60 per cent had experienced discrimination in the workplace with the majority of these (59–60 per cent) identifying the perpetrator as a supervisor (Shift Learning, 2020). In this study women researchers were more likely than men to report they had been bullied (49 per cent compared to 34 per cent) and 44 per cent reported they had been discriminated against. Unfortunately, 28 per cent of respondents reported they would not speak out about bullying and harassment for fear of negative personal consequences:

> This feeling of not wanting to rock the boat was pervasive, and for many it was symptomatic of a culture where bullying was tolerated as long as funding and outputs remained high. Putting your head above the parapet was generally considered highly risky in terms of career implications. (Shift Learning, 2020, p. 30)

Both studies suggest that bullying is positional and related to different forms of socio-structural inequalities (Keashly, 2019; Shift Learning, 2020). Watts (2017) supports this by proposing that bullying is linked to increased management supervision, which in itself is linked to neoliberal managerial ideology that positions workers as untrustworthy (as previously discussed). This perception of management is evident through expectations that staff increasingly acquiesce to 'intensified management demands' (Kirkby & Reiger, 2015, p. 213); an expectation that leads to micromanagement.

Micromanagement is best illustrated in terms of administrivia and proceduralism (Blackmore, 2019b) which serve to keep staff busy. Such busyness limits staff time to reflect on their experiences and to question (Hil, 2012) so that 'the time academics once would have spent interacting with students now gets allocated to new tasks …. Scholars now spend a considerable, and increasing, part of their working day accounting for their activities in the managers' terms' (Watts, 2017, p. 248). Such busyness, micromanaged so that staff cannot avoid the administrivia, results in less and less time available to perform the core work of higher education, with a consequent impact on quality (Spicer, 2018). However, management expectations of output are not reduced to recognise this considerable impost on staff time, and it is my experience that to be perceived as successful, academics must work many more hours than those for which they are paid (Mitchell, 2019). I have sat on many Promotions Committees over the years, and it is my perception that those who are successful in obtaining a promotion are those who work most weekends, over their holiday time and long into the night (or early mornings). It is just not possible to produce the number of quartile 1 journal articles required, obtain high teaching evaluations and engage in leadership and service within the university, the community and the discipline, all of which are the criteria used to evaluate a promotion application, without doing so. I worry about the impact of accepting these expectations, and what that means for young academics beginning their careers. Academia has become not just a calling, but a monster that requires staff to give up much of their private lives. This is further exacerbated by the student as consumer model where responses to student queries are expected to be provided within such a short time frame that does not allow evenings and weekends free of work. The penalty for not doing so is poor evaluations which impact on career progression and workload (with the requirement for written action plans to be provided for poor performance). This is, in itself, a form of bullying in that the expectations placed upon academics go above and beyond what should be expected of a 'normal' person working a 'normal' (as defined by the relevant Enterprise Agreement) working week. Add to that management demands in enterprise bargaining to continually increase the numbers of students taught by a single academic in a calendar year, and I see a nasty form of management bullying that completely disrespects the humanity of staff and positions them as human capital to be exploited as much as possible.

Given such bullying behaviours arise from a combination of expectations established in the figured world, and the ways in which the figured world shapes management style, it is probably unreasonable to suppose that any strategies management put in place to address bullying (as they are required to do by law) will be particularly effective. Indeed, there is research suggesting just this; that interventions designed by management are doomed to be futile (Blackwood, Bentley, & Catley, 2018; Feijó, Gräf, Pearce, & Fassa, 2019; Lipton, 2015; Woodrow & Guest, 2017). My own research (Sims, 2018, 2019a) illustrates this in my figured world.

Recent research indicates that not only are attempts to address bullying often futile, they are hampered by the willingness of management to simply not see their behaviours as bullying (Shift Learning, 2020). In my experience, management demands, no matter how unreasonable they appear to subordinates, are justified by management using the argument of management prerogative (Coyne et al., 2017). The use of the term management prerogative is another form of bullshit language which adds to 'the sadomasochistic dynamic already potentially present in any top-down hierarchical relationship' (Graeber, 2019, p. 122). Management prerogative is used as the explanation for increasingly removing staff from any role in decision making (P. Adams, 2019) and managers are becoming more assertive in using their prerogative in doing so (Blackmore, 2019b). As a consequence of this increasing use, Saunders (2006, p. 15) claims 'literally any comment, advice and action by managers ostensibly designed to improve the "work performance or work-related behaviour" of those they supervise can' now 'be considered legitimate and acceptable.' In other words, management claim the prerogative to identify what is, and is not, reasonable work for their staff even when these claims are contrary to definitions in formal agreements such as enterprise Agreements or relevant workload policies. In my experience, it is considered legitimate and acceptable to refuse to allow academics to take any leave (even a day) during the teaching trimester. It was explained to me that it was reasonable to expect academics to be available to their students every day throughout the entire teaching trimester, and that any leave taken, even one day (which was the claim in the dispute lodged), should be taken in the non-teaching times throughout the year. It is considered legitimate and acceptable to ask staff to spend considerable time (unrecognised in the school workload policy) to develop online practical experiences, then refuse to pay for the additional casual academics needed to deliver these to students. In addition, to then reprimand the staff member concerned for his/her request for casual teaching staff despite his/her demonstrated workload in excess of the school workload policy. The assumption here, as I understand it, was that this staff member was expected to pick up the additional workload of this virtual placement, above and beyond his/her current workload, even though s/he would not normally be expected to cover the workload of student supervision in a non-virtual placement.

Such use of management prerogative is an example of how bullshit language is used to excuse the inexcusable. In this case bullshit language serves to mask 'unsavoury and muscular bullying practices behind the shrouds of HR spin babble' (Smyth, 2017, p. 162) so that for staff, despite legal requirements to address bullying, nothing changes. Staff are increasingly stressed, suffer poor mental and physical health (Morrish, 2019) and performance suffers along with organisational efficiency and productivity.

Performance management

The exceptionally high expectations laid upon staff discussed above arise from the values in the figured world that position continuous improvement as the responsibility of a good neoliberal citizen (Mitchell, 2019; Smyth, 2017). Staff are never thought to be performing their jobs correctly, so they always need to improve their performance (Mayo, 2019; Sims, 2019b). Added to this is the trope that positions staff as untrustworthy, so it is also not surprising that increasingly intrusive and controlling performance management systems are developed.

Internationally, the higher education literature suggests that these performance management systems set expectations and targets that are unattainable for many staff (Morrish, 2019). These systems undermine staff agency and impose greater levels of management control (University of Aberdeen, 2016). They act rather like blunt weapons and 'the very nature of the scrutiny creates a hostile environment for academic freedom' and 'construct[s] academics as liabilities, not as creative institutional asset[s]' (Morrish, 2017, p. 2).

Unfortunately for management, much of the literature suggests that such performance management systems are ineffective, and perhaps even counter-productive (P. Adams, 2019, p. 30) in that they 'not only failed to achieve their potential' but failed to motivate staff as well. In the preface to the Morrish report (Morrish, 2019, p. 4), Mike Thomas, Vice-Chancellor of the University of Central Lancashire, acknowledged the:

> report clearly indicates, with evidence, that directive, performance management approaches are counter-productive to the output, efficiency and effectiveness of the organisation and also to staff well-being and mental health.

Despite the evidence, in my figured world performance management is an requirement that is positioned as functioning as both development and review (Performance Planning Development and Review – PPDR) and it is claimed (<https://www.une.edu.au/staff-current/human-resources/managing-and-recruiting-staff/performance-management/performance-management-framework>):

> Effective performance management will assist UNE to identify, evaluate and develop job performance of staff so that organisational priorities and goals are more effectively achieved, while at the same time benefiting staff through recognising and rewarding their achievements, providing constructive job performance feedback and catering for personal and career development needs.

The process is quite complex (<https://www.une.edu.au/__data/assets/pdf_file/0004/68332/ppdr-flowchart.pdf>). It begins with an initial meeting to discuss performance with the supervisor. The staff member then fills in the online form identifying achievements over the past year and plans for the following year. This form is submitted to the supervisor to add comments and then approve. If the plan is approved then the process ends, which may be of concern where the supervisor has written comments to which the staff member does not agree. Staff can send a request to the supervisor to unlock the form and/or can request, via the form, another meeting with the supervisor to discuss their concerns. These actions, of course, require a supervisor willing to do so and, in my experience, that is not always the case. I remember a situation in which the supervisor rated a colleague as performing unsatisfactorily in teaching based on poor scores from two of five students in a unit evaluation. In doing so, the supervisor both ignored other units taught by this colleague, units with much more positive unit evaluations provided by much larger cohorts of students, and the statistical lack of validity of such a small response rate. Repeated requests to address this concern were ignored by the supervisor and by personnel in human resources. If the supervisor makes changes to the form (for example, the staff member might have requested funds for a particular form of training identified as necessary in the plan and the supervisor may not wish to provide these funds) then the form goes back to the staff member. This process may continue through several iterations until they both agree but there is no process to manage a complete lack of agreement.

In planning for the following year's performance, we are required to address the university's strategic goals: research excellence, outstanding student experience, diversify and grow income, digital dominance, improve operational resilience and create a bold and innovative culture. Some schools and directorates have created options for some of these objectives that staff are required to select and include in their individual plan. We are also required to identify what learning and professional development we propose to undertake in the following year. This has to address the university's core capability framework: shapes and supports strategy, leads and is open to change, acts with courage and integrity, delivers and achieves results, develops and maintains relationships, communicates with influence and occupation specific capabilities (which for academics might include teaching and for professional staff might include trade or professional skills).

I have successfully managed to avoid doing a PPDR for the past several years (for a variety of reasons including particpating in protected industrial action) so I have avoided the horror of having to classify my performance in terms of the university's strategic goals and core capabilities. I can not think how I might possibly assess my performance in terms of enhancing digital dominance (apart from simply using, to the best of my ability, the online learning platform provided) nor how I improved operational resilience (unless critiquing managerial bullshit could be counted as an improvement – though not one I assume management would value). In talking with my colleagues around the campus I have not yet found one person who found the form useful, although conversations with the supervisor were felt to have utility in some cases. However in contrast, I am aware of a number of situations where the PPDR had a major negative impact on staff, increasing stress through feeling targeted by bullying and by natural distress at having achievements overlooked and weaknesses used as weapons of attack. Most colleagues now will not identify areas where they need support in fear that these will be used against them. Rather they learn to use the language of bullshit to talk about their achievements and how they intend to build next year's performance from their strengths. When refusing to participate in the PPDR process was enlivened as a protected industrial action I am sure I heard a sigh of relief sweeping around much of the campus.

Performance management such as this represents in my mind a classic example of how proceduralism has overtaken function and the use of bullshit language to hide the worthlessness of the whole process. It is rare in my experience for staff to identify any benefits from the process as it stands (which is why staff briefed the union to make this a key element to address in the enterprise bargaining round). The bullshit language used in the system is obscure with no conceptual value. As a consequence it is difficult for staff to match the realities of their figured world with the figured world portrayed in the process. This use of:

> bullshit disempowers those who use or are exposed to it. By being both useless and ambiguous, bullshit weakens the connection between participants, language and reality … language emptied of any meaningful connection with people's experience is a tool to foster obedience. (Contandriopoulos, 2019, p. 3)

PPDR in my figured world is no longer perceived by staff as a development process, but as a process used by management to impose control and conformity. My point is summarized in the manifesto developed by the University of Aberdeen (2016, p. 4; point 15):

> Performance management undermines professionalism in assuming that scholars are not motivated by a desire to advance knowledge in their fields but are responsive only to threats and incentives issued by managers. It undermines collegiality in attaching these threats and incentives to targets that bear no relation to the contribution that individuals make to the communities of scholarship to which they belong.

In addressing this concern, the manifesto proposed that in the university they will (p. 1):

> Restore the trust that underpins both professionalism and collegiality, by removing the conditions of line and performance management, and of surveillance, which lead to its erosion.

Managers are the university

Increasingly I see managers taking over the identity of the university and excluding other stakeholders. The University of New England Act 1993 – As at 22 November 2018 (<http://www6.austlii.edu.au/cgi-bin/viewdb/au/legis/nsw/consol_act/uonea1993281/>) in Section 4 defines 'The University' as consisting of its Council, convocation, alumni, staff, graduates and students.' However, all stakeholders of the university are more often excluded and the term 'The University' is increasingly being used to refer solely to management. For example, the Vice Chancellor's Communiqué sent to all staff on 18 September 2019 (available publicly on <https://us3.campaign-archive.com/?u=0b102b47b45c5ad5bb5ffac2a&id=11a3f89c75>: p.3 of downloaded version) claimed (my emphasis):

> the NTEU's tactic to withdraw labour for a small, random fraction of each day makes it almost impossible for *the University* to effectively manage alternate modes of support. It also makes it very difficult for *the University* to act fairly in identifying the amount of work not performed for the purposes of issuing a notice to reduce payment ... The UNE position has been clearly stated and there have been numerous opportunities over the intervening two year period for a meaningful open debate.

This email makes it clear that management perceive themselves as 'the university'; it is not the responsibility of students, graduates, convocation nor alumni to manage a response to protected industrial action, nor is it council, convocation, alumni, all staff and students who have 'clearly stated' a position in relation to the issues of dispute. This is management speaking for management alone yet claiming to speak for 'the University', emphasizing again a clear them and us position being taken.

Shore (2010, p. 26) agrees, noting:

> University management teams have not only arrogated to themselves the role of 'speaking for the university'; increasingly, they now claim to be the University, and relegate staff, alumni and students to the role of 'stakeholders' – along with students, parents, industry and government.

Connell (2019a) notes the same, pointing out that management take-over is reflected in the annexation of decision-making power. What this suggests to me is that, intentionally or not, management in their language are clearly stating what they believe; that they are totally responsible for running the university, making decisions and that the past practices of collegial governance are, in their eyes, dead and gone. In the figured world of managers, such a position is a key element of neoliberal managerialism, in particular the 'reassertion of ruling class authority' (Means & Slater, 2019, p. 164). Managers claim more and more power (Hil, 2012; Spicer, 2018) and having obtained that power, continue to act in ways that maintain it (Watts, 2017).

> *'Efficiency' has come to mean vesting more and more power to managers, supervisors, and other presumed 'efficiency experts,' so that actual producers have almost zero autonomy. At the same time, the ranks and orders of managers seem to reproduce themselves endlessly.* (Graeber, 2019, p. 178)

In an interesting dig at this usurpation of power, Shore and Wright (2019, p. 8) argue: 'managers and administrators have usurped power in what were formerly more collegial, self-governing institutions. Yet many of these managers would not succeed as professionals in industry.'

In its manifesto the University of Aberdeen (2016, pp. 8, point 30) note the suggested strategy to address this involves appointing leaders not managers. These leaders are expected to be part of the community and are chosen by the community; 'not by shadowy committees whose members may have little experience of higher education, nor by firms of head-hunters which have their own business interests at heart.'

Managers and post-truth

In staking their claim for power, management are increasingly using the language of post-truth, the language I am calling bullshit. Language is powerful and is used to reconfigure academic work to enforce 'compliance and docility' (Manathunga & Bottrell, 2019b, p. 298) re-inforcing management's annexation of power (Contandriopoulos, 2019; C. Wright, 2019). Explaining this point, Apple (2017, p. 148) claims that:

> the power of particular groups who understand that if they can change the basic ways we think about our society and its institutions – and especially our place in these institutions – these groups can create a set of policies that will profoundly benefit them more than anyone else.

The language of bullshit used by managers is 'fraught with power relations. What "the market wants" tends to mean what corporations and their bosses want' (Monbiot, 2016, p. 6). Take for example a recent email from the Vice Chancellor that argued: 'many of our Academic staff have indicated their support for a new EB workloads model based on the now accepted sector norm of an hours-based workload model' (Vice Chancellor's Communiqué, sent to all staff on 18 September 2019, available publicly on <https://us3. campaign-archive.com/?u=0b102b47b45c5ad5bb5ffac2a&id=11a3f 89c75>, p.2 of downloaded version). The email went on to refer readers to a site where the survey results were provided. Anyone bothering to click on the link was taken to a site that presented the *UNE Staff Enterprise Bargaining Survey Academic Staff Results 2017*. This document did not have anything about a new workload model nor any question in it that could be construed as asking about support for a new model. Luckily, I downloaded this document from the site on the day the email was sent out because two days later the link in the email no longer took me to this site but to another document entitled: *Addendum to VC Communique – Wednesday, 18 September 2019*. This document argued in support of an hours-based workload model using as evidence, the percentage of staff who, in the survey, had claimed that the current model did not accurately reflect their work and the percentage who felt the current model was not applied equitably across the university. Clearly it is in the interests of management to seek an hours-based model, and my calculations of workload based on the proposed model indicate that the majority of academics would experience an increase in workload should this go ahead. However, this is not acknowledged in management's document. Rather the proposed new model is claimed to improve flexibility, innovation, agility, transparency, equity and sustainability.

Language such as this is hard to challenge as it addresses key elements of our work as academics. 'The strategic and rhetorical application of euphemisms creates a situation where it is difficult to disagree with the apparent sentiments' (Taylor, 2003, p. 10) of terms such as 'modern, efficient, smart, necessary' (Connell, 2019b, p. vi) but the reality in my experience is the opposite: old fashioned, stupid and unnecessary. However, bullshit language is specifically designed to obfuscate meaning (Gaztambide-Fernández, 2011) and its use has become the new norm (Connell, 2019a). In becoming so, bullshit creates a context where regard for truth is no longer important whilst, simultaneously, giving the impression that a profound message is being conveyed (Christensen et al., 2019; Frankfurt, 2005).

Bullshit language not just risks the integrity of communication, it also impairs ability to think (Klikauer & Tabassum, 2019; Spicer, 2018). In his classic work, Frankfurt (2005, p. 63) wrote: 'Bullshit is unavoidable when circumstances require someone to talk without knowing what he is talking about.' Recently, for example, management responded to protected industrial action taken by staff (refusal to respond to student queries on the online platform and student emails) by granting all students across the university a seven working day extension. This was justified as an attempt to mitigate any impact on students. This caused immense confusion for students and staff, none of whom were clear if the seven days were actually seven days or seven working days. Academic staff received many emails from students seeking clarification which ate up a lot of their time, and one staff member was actually the target of a formal student complaint which alleged the uncertainty impacted on performance in the assignment. No one in management thought about the implications of this for the submission of end of trimester results. The likely outcome was that few academics were able to complete marking in time, meaning the majority of results remained outstanding. Not only does the proportion of outstanding results reflect negatively on academic staff performance (it is one of the indicators used to assess quality teaching), the process to subsequently amend marks is particularly cumbersome. This process requires a form to be completed for each individual student for each individual result, the handling of which engaged professional staff in huge amounts of work, reducing their available time for other tasks. As identified by Spicer (2018, p. 14) bullshit provides management with opportunities to propose 'comfortable, yet ultimately empty solutions.'

Speaking the language of bullshit is an important skill that managers need to cement their position in the figured world of management. This is a process very similar to that described in Gaztambide-Fernández (2011)'s research where the boys attending elite schools learned how to use the 'right' language to demonstrate their belonging. Once managers belong in their group, they internalise the values associated with management (in my case neoliberal managerialism) and use these values to shape their behaviour. Their perceptions of the world around them are also influenced by their figured world. Ball (2017) talks about how these values create a kind of filter bubble, which shapes their perceptions to match their understandings of the world in which they operate. Loyalty to the group is then demonstrated by attacks on those who are not part of the group as these behaviours serve to signal how thoroughly one belongs in the group. Ultimately group members are so successful in teaching themselves to perceive their world view, their beliefs and their behaviours as correct, they persuade themselves that the bullshit they speak is the truth (Davis, 2017). Many are 'blind to the bullshit they create' (Graeber, 2019, p. 65). Thus, it is quite possible that the manager who claimed an uncapped, hours-based workload model would create growth, flexibility and still be supportive of staff wellbeing (as identified in the previously referenced *Addendum to VC Communique – Wednesday, 18 September 2019*) may genuinely believe this to be the case despite all the evidence to the contrary (a similar kind of blindness to reality is discussed in Spicer, 2018). The flip side of this is of course 'By your choice of bullshit, you tell me a lot about who you are, or aspire to be' (Ball, 2017, p. 111).

Summary

The figured world of managers is one in which privilege and value are identified by concrete indicators such as salary levels. There is little evidence to support a claim that those filling these positions are worth the money they receive, however there is an implicit assumption that, given neoliberalism equates worth with money, these salaries are necessary to maintain desired inequity between managers and workers. The figured world of managers is maintained by those who are in the in-group through the use of bullshit language which obscures what they do. This bullshit language serves as a marker of identity and belonging; a fluent speaker of bullshit is clearly worthy of belonging in the ranks of management. Bullshit language also obscures the conceptually empty words and phrases used, hiding their lack of meaning under a cover of apparent profundity. Unfortunately, management actions arising from bullshit words and thinking demonstrate clearly a lack of understanding of the figured world of staff and of the realities of core service delivery.

Those who identify as belonging to the figured world of management not only display their belonging through their fluency in bullshit, they also learn to behave in certain ways. It is not clear if particular personality traits predispose their possessors to succeed in management positions or if becoming attached to the figured world of management reinforces certain personality traits. Perhaps the influences are bi-directional. Irrespective of how the causality operates, it is clear that the figured world of managers positions its inhabitants to act with decreasing levels of empathy and increasing levels of narcissism. On average, managers tend to exhibit increasing levels of psychopathic personality disorder, and there is even some evidence that increased identification with neoliberal managerialism may increase the risk of corrupt conduct (in particular where economic decisions trump moral ones). Managers exhibiting extreme forms of these traits are exhibiting dark leadership.

Managers act out the scripts expected of them to cement their belonging in their figured world. These scripts are more and more often perceived by those on the receiving end as bullying. Targets of bullying demonstrate increasingly higher rates of stress, along with mental and physical health problems (Shift Learning, 2020), however in the figured world of managers, these problems are perceived as a lack of staff resiliency. Processes to address bullying, required by law and supposedly designed to focus on staff wellbeing, are operationalized by managers functioning within this framework and are almost universally ineffective. In the bullshit speak of the managerial world, their behaviour is justified on the basis of managerial prerogative. They have the right to demand staff compliance in any context related to the performance of work and staff need to learn how to comply.

The focus on ensuring staff compliance is reinforced by the imposition of performance management systems. These systems align staff performance to organisation goals and objectives and function to further oppress staff and limit their agency. Bullshit language used to define organisation goals and objectives, along with capability frameworks identifying desired staff attributes, make it extremely difficult to translate expectations from the figured world of managers into the figured world of staff, further reinforcing management lack of trust in staff and cementing their belief that staff need to be more and more closely controlled.

The ultimate bullshit in my eyes is management annexation of the university. Whilst legislation defines 'the university' as a combination of staff, students, council, convocation and alumni, increasingly management are claiming that they are 'the university'. In claiming this position management are reinforcing the neoliberal managerial figured world which reifies those who are elite, and progressively disenfranchises and oppresses workers. In an interview, Tim Ingold states: 'The educational environments in which we work are increasingly dogmatic and oppressive, and worse still, dogma and oppression are being delivered in the name of freedom and creativity' (Campbell, 2018, p. 4). The figured world of managers is one in which power is annexed and exercised over staff. Bullshit language is used to justify this process, and to coerce staff into accepting this as natural and right.

CHAPTER 6

The figured world of followership

The Course Co-ordinator of a particular discipline, Taylor, was notified by a manager, Campbell, that a private service provider operating in the sector had contacted the university. The contact person from the private service provider was Eddie. In this sector the federal government had, some years previously, set an agenda that strongly encouraged staff working in the sector to upgrade from a vocational qualification to a university degree. Eddie wanted to talk to the relevant people in the university to explore possibilities of an agreement that would support a largish cohort of staff from his/her organisation through their studies to upgrade their qualifications. Taylor and team had previously been approached by other private service providers in the sector and were clear that all students enrolled in the course would receive the support needed within the normal parameters of what was possible to offer. Support for students in each unit of study was tailored to the learning requirements of each student, as much as possible within the rigid requirements of the university and the external course accreditation agencies. All students in a unit had access to the teaching staff, and were able to seek from them what support they needed. There is no capacity within the system for a particular cohort of students to be offered anything beyond this, and to offer additional support to some, and not all, students in a unit would be inequitable. Taylor indicated willingness to liaise with Eddie. However, Campbell insisted on remaining the point of contact. Some weeks later Taylor and Eddie managed to have a teleconference only to find that sometime in the week before Campbell and two other managers had had a conversation with Eddie. In that teleconference Eddie reported to Taylor that there were a number of issues that this team of managers were unable to answer, and hoped that Taylor would be able to do so.

Taylor was annoyed that this conversation had been undertaken without informing him/her and felt that this portrayed a poor public image for the university. Taylor shared with Campbell how this was perceived by him/herself and the team s/he represented: 'this yet again demonstrates a lack of effective communication within management and a lack of trust in and respect for staff with relevant expertise' (permission received to share).

Campbell's response indicated that the initial meeting was, in his/her view, a simple meet and greet, and that s/he was sorry that Taylor felt communication was ineffective, but s/he had fully intended to pass on the information at some point. Other team members felt embarrassed with the inefficient image they felt this presented to the world. There were also feelings of anger. For example, one wrote: 'More and more I see people pretending they are involved in things because they are in management, but really, they are just doing nothing and sometimes being detrimental. It ticks a box for them and justifies their role' (permission received to share).

The frustration and anger experienced by this team is, in my experience, no longer an uncommon experience in the figured world of followers. Neoliberal managerialism positions workers as untrustworthy, and in need of extensive supervision. This inferior positioning is reflected in an increasing salary gap between workers and managers (for example, the highest paid executive in Australia is Alan Joyce of Qantas whose $23.9 million salary is 275 times greater than the average wage: Khadem, 2019b). It is also evident in the apparent lack of awareness of managers of how the ways they continue to reinforce their positions of privilege are perceived by those they are supposed to be managing. Whilst the expectations of followers in this figured world are clear, the experience of followership itself has yet to receive much research attention (Morris, 2015; Prilipko, 2019), particularly so in the higher education sector where academics are more likely to have expectations of a certain level of autonomy over their work. This chapter addresses followership in my figured world, as illustrated in Figure 5.

Followership

In the western world the idea of followership tends to be associated with somewhat negative qualities such as passivity, lack of intelligence and perhaps laziness (Prilipko, 2019): 'individuals who lack the physical,

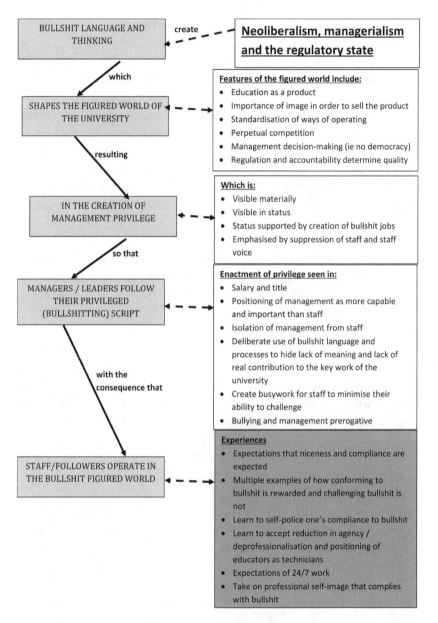

Figure 5. Fitting followership into the conceptual framework

psychological, or social capital to be leaders themselves are more likely to emerge as followers' (Bastardoz & Van Vugt, 2019, p. 81). Rather tongue-in-cheek, Kelley (2008, p. 6) writes that followership is commonly compared 'to sled dogs whose destiny is always to look at the rear end of the dog in front of them, but never to see the wider horizon or make the decisions of the lead dog.' Making the point more strongly, Linstead, Maréchal, and Griffin (2014) refer to followership as a modern form of slavery. Followership is positioned as the flip side of leadership; those with sufficient intelligence and drive should aspire to leadership positions whereas others remain as followers because they lack these characteristics. As a consequence of this negative view, much of the research around followership only addresses the concept in the context of how followership informs leadership. For example, Milosevic et al. (2019) argued understanding followership is an essential prerequisite to understanding effective leadership. Kock, Mayfield, Mayfield, Sexton, and De La Garza (2019) argued effective leaders were those who demonstrated sufficient empathy towards their followers in order to increase follower job satisfaction.

It is clear that leaders could not be leaders without followers thus followership ought to be accorded the same importance as leadership (Nawaz Khan, Halim Busari, & Mariam Abdullah, 2019). Pietraszewski (2019) goes a step further, arguing that both leadership and followership are inevitable elements of human groups. Followership behaviour serves an important purpose in facilitating successful group participation (Bastardoz & Van Vugt, 2019). In other words, followership is not just the characteristics of individuals, it is a process that operates in an inter-personal context; something that people do together (Morris, 2015). In the process of so 'doing', both followers and leaders co-construct their identities (Nawaz Khan et al., 2019) in a context that shapes their expectations of each other.

Given the dynamic nature of the co-construction of leadership and followership, and the influence of the context on shaping expectations of each other, it is no surprise that there are a range of different definitions of followership in the literature. For example, Morris (2015) reviews different ideas that share in common the proposition that followership involves a choice; followers have freedom to decide who they will follow and how they wish to position themselves in their followership role. Padilla, Hogan, and Kaiser (2007), identified two types of choices offered to followers of toxic leaders resulting in two different sorts of followers: conformers and colluders. Colluders comply in order to gain something for themselves. In contrast, conformers do as they are told because they are frightened to not do so. In many organisations, followers might not have a choice about who they follow, but they may have more control over how they will follow. In my figured world, with its multiple layers of hierarchy, it is possible to argue that, whilst I have to follow the directions of each and every one of the managers 'above' me in the hierarchy, I may choose to follow different managers in different ways.

Stanley (2017) takes a broader perspective, presenting a range of follower types, where it is assumed that followers make a choice in relation to the way they wish to play their followership role, including:

- Participant – those who are actively involved in the joint action; Jin, McDonald III, Park, and Trevor Yu (2019) suggest those with a deep committment to their profession are more likely to put up with things they don't like in their environment just so they can get on with what is important to them,
- Pessimist – those who do not want to engage in any change,
- Passenger – those who are not engaged and do not wish to be,
- Pig – those who are only there for what they can get for themselves,
- Prisoner – those who are there but not by choice.

In my context, it is possible that my colleagues are present in the workplace for all of these reasons. Some are totally committed to higher education and will do whatever is necessary to enable them to get on with their work (whether their focus is teaching, research or service or any combination of these three). Others (such as myself) actively resist the neoliberal managerial changes being imposed and try to fight for other alternatives whilst still trying to meet personal standards of work productivity. A number do not want to know what is going on, do not want to engage in anything other than what they need to do to carry on unnoticed. There are some who are strongly career-minded; who will do whatever it takes to get the next article published, to get a good student evaluation and to succeed in the next promotion. Finally, there are those who see their work as a way to generate income; necessary but not particularly enjoyable. In my experience this latter category is unusual in academia; many academics have a significant commitment to their profession that enables them to overlook (or consider less important) neoliberal managerial attacks on their professionalism.

Assuming that staff in higher education move into the higher education sector with some kind of idea of how they expect to enact their followership roles, the context in which they find themselves working then acts on these personal models to shape their experiences. As I have discussed in previous chapters, neoliberalism reifies the divide between the elite and the workers, positioning workers as untrustworthy, lazy consumers who would prefer 'a strong leader to save them rather than make the effort themselves' (Ball, 2017, p. 175). Their laziness leads them to accept what they are told without bothering to check information, which is the underpinning problem Ball (2017) sees with our post-truth world.

Thus workers may enter an employment context with an expectation that their followership role might require of them characteristics such as integrity, dependability, good communication skills, industry, and enthusiasm (Da'as & Zibenberg, 2019) only to find that the ideal followership role is constituted rather differently. How this tension is resolved impacts on the way in which the followership role is enacted by each person. In his ground-breaking research on followership, Kelley (1988) suggested that followers select an appropriate level of activity and critical thinking in performing their followership roles. It is the interaction of these characteristics, operating within the work context, that determine if followers can be categorized as yes people; alienated followers; survivors; or effective followers.

This suggests that followership is about playing a role, which may or may not mesh well with individual self-identity and may or may not mesh with the professional identity carried into the workplace. Obviously the closer the match, the more natural the followership role will feel, and perhaps the less damaging performing that role might be to the follower. Authentic followership occurs when the values and beliefs of followers actually match those of their employing organisation and form the basis of their experiences at work (Morris, 2015). Authenticity itself 'can be characterized as the unobstructed operation of one's true, or core, self in one's daily enterprise' (Kernis, 2003, p. 1). Nawaz Khan et al. (2019) place this idea in a constructivist frame. They argue that the values and beliefs of followers interact with those of managers. When the role granted to a manager by followers meets the manager's expectations, and the role claimed by followers for themselves meets the manager's expectations, positive workplace culture results and both leadership and followership can be successfully enacted. Where authentic leadership and followership are enacted, both roles are underpinned by self-awareness, and a commitment to ethics and morals (Morris, 2015). Kernis (2003) adds lack of bias, relational transparency, and authentic behaviour to the characteristics of authentic followership. All of these are characteristics that, I argue, are not valued in neoliberal understandings of followership, and thus are neither expected, encouraged nor rewarded.

In my figured world and my experience, when the claiming and granting do not match, both leadership and followership roles are in conflict, with a consequent impact on productivity and workplace wellbeing, for both managers and workers. In extreme circumstances, it appears that followers may contribute in some way to the establishment and maintenance of dark and/or toxic leadership (Milosevic et al., 2019). However, there is also evidence that follower behaviours can reduce the negative impact of dark leadership (Braun et al., 2019a). Followers can engage in behaviour such as challenging the assumptions that are taken for granted, asking questions about anything they feel is suspicious and both naming and challenging wrong-doing (Fraher, 2016). Of course, all of these actions have consequences, the least of which is a private warning to tread carefully.

In my experiences of followership, the role expected of me is one in which I am required to comply (with policies, to managers' orders) and that it is my responsibility to ensure that I do so. However, given I am not to be trusted, my compliance must be monitored; most often by professional staff and/or academic supervisors appointed at a lower grade than mine. My followership is not about what I think and feel; it is about a daily demonstration of my compliance. I operate within a hierarchy that is established separately to academic appointment level; rather it is a managerial imposition where people have been placed in various roles in order to supervise academic activity. In my experience, my followership is about my subordination to those who have been placed 'above' me in a managerial hierarchy. As a subordinate, I am placed in a passive position with no power. Definitions that co-locate followership with choice are not definitions that meet my experience. If I want decision-making power then I ought to apply for one of the many supervisory managerial roles that make up the hierarchy in my university. If I chose to remain in a followership position then I need to accept that I can, and should, be 'bossed around' by anyone located in the management hierarchy above me (which is everyone in that hierarchy). I need to respond to this 'bossing' with grace and respect, and I need to accept that I will never perform my job satisfactorily and that I therefore need to continually improve my performance.

Be nice

As a compliant neoliberal citizen, I am expected to accept my lowly position in the hierarchy with grace. The alternative is to choose to assert myself to signal my suitability to join management ranks (through enthusiastic conformity). Having previously operated in these managerial ranks, my 'choice' is clear to me: no way do I want to move back into positions where I feel I cannot perform authentically, and where I am expected to enforce procedures I feel are dehumanizing, disrespectful and counter-productive to the delivery of the core work of the university. I hold to my position despite being told by one senior manager I am an immense disappointment to him/her, and despite being told by another that it would be a joke were I to be considered. I am expected to accept these kinds of comments, and to subjugate my feelings and my ability to think critically so that I can simply get along (similar to the non-thinking compliance described in Alvesson & Spicer, 2016).

Neoliberalism positions workers in subordinate positions to managerial power and propounds 'the idea that dutiful submission even to meaningless work under another's authority is a form of moral self-discipline that makes you a better person' (Graeber, 2019, p. 94). A better person is one who is 'nice' when conforming (Furedi, 2017) in order to signal to management (Davis, 2017) s/he deserves to belong in their elite ranks. In effect, obedience, conformity and niceness are rewarded (Saunders, 2006; Smyth, 2017) despite the fear, cowardice, cynicism and sycophancy that this generates. Movement into the elite ranks is often dependent on the extent to which the person is liked by management (D. Ross et al., 2020) and the extent to which the person has already demonstrated through their compliant, nice behaviour, that s/he belongs. Challenging management or engaging in any form of dissent has a ruinous impact on career progression.

Clear demonstrations of the dangerousness of dissent (Giroux, 2015; McNally, 2018) help create a climate of fear that makes it more difficult for workers to speak out. Non-compliant bodies 'will be refused and rendered aberrant' (Morrish, 2018, p. 2). For example, in our 2018 school review, the review panel recommended that those staff who did not genuinely engage in whatever was done to rebuild school culture should be offered a voluntary separation package. Cynicism as to the meaning of the word 'voluntary' was evident in ensuing conversations, with definitions including 'You! Go' and animated discussions speculating on who it might be that management wanted to get rid of the most. Despite the light-hearted humour characterizing these conversations, the impact was particularly negative. Subsequent to this document being released I was party to a number of informal conversations where colleagues told me they felt even more frightened than before that they could be targeted by members of management if they indicated any sign of dissent with any action. Colleagues told me they not only felt frightened, they also felt silenced and disempowered.

Whilst the role of public intellectual is one traditionally associated with academia (Edgar & Edgar, 2019), in our neoliberal managerial figured world, many academics are now not just silent within the workplace, but also publicly silent (Kenway et al., 2015). There appears to me to be growing pressure to require employees to present a positive image of their organisation not only in public, but within the organisation itself. A relentless focus on the positive, whilst important to prevent wallowing in negativity and hopelessness, poses risks when anxious avoidance of any form of negativity obscures problems. Risk is compounded when bullshit rhetoric is used to 'speak up' the positives in ways that hide the meaninglessness of proposed goals and actions. Spicer (2018) suggests that our cultural desire to be polite prevents us from challenging this kind of neoliberal managerial bullshit. He argues: '[q]uestioning bullshit, is a sure way to lose friends and alienate people' (p. 88) and so 'we try to not embarrass others, risk damaging social relationships (p. 91). You can be cynical about management bullshit all you want in private, but in public you need to pretend you are all signed up' (p. 93). Unfortunately this silence has the effect of supporting the status quo (Ball, 2017; Hil, 2012). I remember once collating comments from a group discussion about a particular proposed change. When it was time to put names on the feedback document very few of the participants in the discussion were willing to do so, even though the discussion held was in response to a call for feedback from management.

Reinforcing this in my figured world are continual reminders that staff are expected to exercise their academic freedom judiciously. Staff are required to 'act in the best interest of the University and value the University's reputation' and to '[n]ever behaving in a way that may damage the University's reputation, whilst representing the University' (Code of Conduct, downloaded 26 September 2019 from <https://policies.une.edu. au/document/view-current.php?id=140>). Whilst this does not prevent staff from commenting in their private citizen roles, there remains great concern that the boundary between private and public lives is increasingly blurred (Taberner, 2018), so that fear of reprisal acts as a barrier preventing many from sharing their concerns in any public arena.

The image of academia (as a place where intellectuals gather) suggests that a university environment is one in which it might be expected staff would regularly challenge bullshit (Christensen et al., 2019). However, the ability to do so is not just limited by fear of reprisal but by inability to recognise bullshit. In particular, I argue, those who have adopted neo-liberal managerial values are much more likely to blind themselves to the meaningless and deliberate obfuscation inherent in the bullshit language they hear. It would be a rare academic who would deliberately argue that low-quality teaching was perfectly acceptable. A sensible academic, how-ever, might well argue for the need to lower quality in order to survive horrendous teaching loads. Quality and excellence of student experience are what all engaged in higher education wish to deliver so it is particularly difficult to challenge bullshit speak that identifies these as management's priority. In contrast, management actions that focus on increasing teaching loads and decreasing the duration of teaching time (semesters of 12 weeks to trimesters of eight weeks to proposed terms of six weeks all available for full-time study, for example), indicate that the reality of the figured world of staff is very different from the bullshit claims made in the figured world of management.

In management's figured world, the perceived barrier to quality teaching is not their unrealistic actions, but the laziness and incompetence of staff. In the figured world of management, it appears completely reasonable that an academic can mark 200 large assignments, taking up to an hour each, in a two-week period; a situation created by management who unilaterally gave every student an extension because of industrial action, thereby decimating the carefully planned marking schedule set up by this particular staff member. At a surface, uncritical level, management's action in granting a universal extension appears kind. In the figured world of staff who have to manage the workload, the action was perceived as insane and a reflection of a complete lack of understanding of the reality of the figured world in which staff operate. In response to this imposition, most staff simply worked longer hours and did their best to rearrange their marking schedules to ensure as many assignments were marked as possible in the shorter timeline available to them between new submission dates and due date for final marks. Most were far too busy to challenge management's decision or to be able to provide feedback as to the impact on them, and the consequent impact on students whose assignments could not be marked in time, and whose final results were therefore significantly delayed. In this case busyness and staff niceness precluded challenging the bullshit rhetoric that positioned management's move as supportive of students. In this post-truth world, not challenging bullshit tends to result in the bullshit gaining ascendancy in people's thinking (Ball, 2017). What is not challenged and debated is, more and more, being perceived as 'the truth.' Being nice, not challenging bullshit creates a narrative that drives the figured worlds of management and staff, and without an alternative narrative, what is, continues to be.

Accept your lack of agency and power

Neoliberalism creates a figured world in which its subjects experience the destruction of 'social responsibility and critique, that invites a mindless, consumer-oriented individualism to flourish, and kills off conscience' (Davies, 2005, p. 6). Living immersed in this figured world impacts on our identity (Malakyan, 2019). Followers in my figured world of neoliberal managerialism are positioned as weak, obedient, and passive. When people are subject to these values, and experience the behaviours arising from them, they internalise this oppression and it becomes part of their perceptions of who they are (Freire, 1973). Research suggests that higher levels of stress are associated with this lack of value ascribed to one's work and concomitant poor identity, and that these particular triggers result in stress that is more harmful than other forms of stress (Kinman & Wray, 2020). Further, once this identity is established, people then act in ways congruent with their self-identity, thus, as Freire argued many years ago, systems of oppression become self-sustaining. As (Davies, 2005, p. 7) claimed, this becomes visible in behaviours that derive from:

> a smallminded moralism that rewards the attack of each small powerless person on the other, and it shuts down creativity. It draws on and exacerbates a fear of difference and rewards a rampant, consumerist, competitive individualism.

Whilst modern identity theory suggests identities are fluid, and often change in different contexts (for example one might be passive at work, but a leader on the sports field), what remains clear is that the figured world of followership in my context reinforces the hierarchical nature of worker subjugation.

In that context the kinds of follower identity originally discussed by Kelley (1988, 2008) over 30 years ago still remain relevant. Kelley categorized types of followership across two dimensions: a continuum between active and passive, and a continuum between independent critical thinking and dependent, uncritical thinking as illustrated in Figure 6. Followers identified as independent critical thinkers are able to provide constructive criticism, and do not simply follow blindly. They tend to be enthusiastic,

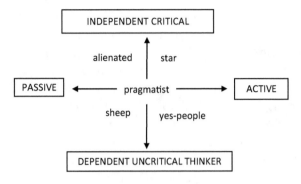

Figure 6. Dimensions of Kelley (1988)'s model of followership

creative, energetic and more productive. Actively engaged followers feel they belong in the organisation and engage in decision-making. Engagement is important, as without this, followers are more likely to comply without thought. Alienated followers are those who resist change, are likely to be critical of managers but they are often passive in their resistance, not willing to move outside their comfort zones to engage in more activist rebellion. Star followers are those who place the organisation (or their professional standards) above the requirements of their managers, and who therefore are able to challenge managers when they think what they are doing is not right for the organisation. Star followers may well be the best support for managers, but they may also be managers' worst nightmares. In contrast, pragmatic followers observe but may not always act. They tend to think: 'If I got all excited every time there was a new leader or a change of direction, my wheels would be spinning constantly. Leaders come and go. New visions come and go. If I just sit here and wait it out, I won't have to do all that work' (Kelley, 2008, p. 8).

The kinds of followership required of staff in my figured world are those in the lower quarters of Kelley's model: sheep and yes-people. Both these types are uncritical thinkers so will blindly follow instructions. Sheep particularly like decisions to be made for them. These are the people who stick rigidly to a proforma; step-by-step guides. I am reminded of a manager who once argued equity requires everyone to be treated exactly the same. Therefore it was utterly appropriate to refuse allow an international staff member permission to travel, in work time, to attend a compulsory visa health check in an approved medical centre five hours away because other staff members (Australians who did not require a visa health check to remain in their job) did not attend medical appointments in work time. Yes-people, the other form of followership, are often energetic in following out their orders, but again do not think for themselves, so on completion of a task will ask what needs to be done next.

Kelley's work suggests that managers are influenced by followers' behaviours. Where managers perceive their followers to be incompetent they are more likely to micromanage. The imbalance of power between managers and followers reinforces this perception of incompetence and untrustworthiness (Morris, 2015) which then, in turn, reinforces the growing distance between the groups. These combine to instil a sense of powerlessness in workers who often report feeling as if they are owned by the organisation, under the control of others and forced to obey (Morris, 2015).

Being placed in this position, followers are sometimes forced to choose between their requirement to obey and their own values (or conscience). Over 50 years ago, Milgram's (1963, 1965) shock experiments demonstrated how much humans are motivated to be obedient, even when their compliance goes against their values. Baronce (2015) suggests that this compliance is linked to the authority that is located in the leadership role. Followers assume that their leaders know what they are doing and therefore they are not expected to think for themselves, rather they simply follow their leaders' orders. I have heard colleagues excuse what appears to be an incomprehensible management requirement by assuming that management have access to more information than they, and that the requirement must make sense in the light of that unknown information. The lack of management understanding of the reality in which the requirement has to be enacted is not considered by these colleagues to be important. Thus, the context is particularly important in establishing role for participants. In the figured world of followers, compliance is expected, enforced and accepted as the natural way of things. Not thinking can make it easier to follow orders, resulting in the kind of functional stupidity so well described in Alvesson and Spicer (2016). I see this operating in my figured world. For example, there remain a large number of staff who believe that it is appropriate to trust management to set their workloads and that enforceable, easily identifiable caps are not needed. This belief operates in spite of a case taken to the Fair Work Commission challenging management in one area where all academics were forced to work to the maximum allowable teaching load in defiance of the relevant School Workload Policies that should have prevented this.

Manage yourself

Having accepted the identity associated with followership, followers then shape their behaviour to be congruent with their imposed identity in order to get along in their figured world. One of the key elements of neoliberalism is its strong emphasis on individualism and the responsibility of individuals to manage their lives. As Verhaeghe (2014, p. 2) explains:

> Our society constantly proclaims that anyone can make it if they just try hard enough, all the while reinforcing privilege and putting increasing pressure on its overstretched and exhausted citizens. An increasing number of people fail, feeling humiliated, guilty and ashamed. We are forever told that we are freer to choose the course of our lives than ever before, but the freedom to choose outside the success narrative is limited. Furthermore, those who fail are deemed to be losers or scroungers, taking advantage of our social security system.

Followers are placed in an invidious position in that they are expected to accept the followership role as defined in their figured world, yet are also expected to strive to be successful; to make something of themselves. Inequity is thrust into their attention daily as they witness the privileges their managers take for granted, and their own feelings of powerlessness are exacerbated as they have to seek permission to undertake core elements of their work. This daily exposure to inequality, coupled with their imposed role in the figured world which requires them to both accept their followership status yet seek to improve themselves, leads to feelings of anger, disenchantment (Samier, 2018), and often disengagement. Hartwich and

Becker (2019) introduce the concept of anomie to describe the focus on individualism, materialism and economic success at the cost of morals and social engagement. Anomie is most likely to be evident, they argue, in contexts where there are restricted legitimate means to move into positions of privilege. This is particularly evident in my figured world where the route to promotion requires demonstration, over a sustained period of time, that one is functioning consistently, across all domains of academic work, at the level to which one is aspiring. This includes student evaluations of teaching that are consistently high, research outputs that demonstrate an increasing trajectory of achievement with at least some top quartile-ranked journal publications, and service to the university as well as high profile service to the profession and/or community. Requirements for performance at an above average level across multiple domains means that most will not meet the criteria. The very meaning of the word average means that half the staff evaluated cannot be above average even though their performance may be perfectly acceptable or even exemplary. Thus, a large proportion of the workforce are placed in a position where they feel their work is not valued. Unfortunately, under neoliberalism the distress this causes is seen to be the problem of the individuals feeling this way, who supposedly are responsible for fixing their own problems (Bettache & Chiu, 2019). Failing is their own fault for not trying sufficiently hard (Blackmore, 2019a), and critiquing this inequity is also seen as an excuse for not trying sufficiently hard (the term snowflake can be heard here).

Under this regime of individualism, followers are not expected to rely on management for support (Datta & Chakraborty, 2018). Rather, in attempts to 'fix' their inadequacies, followers are expected to invest their time in self-improvement. Thus the ideal follower must (Stanley, 2017):

- Learn all s/he can about the organisation,
- Take responsibility for ensuring their work contributes towards organisational goals (noting that the performance management system in my figured world requires staff to link their activities and goals to the organisation's strategic plan),
- Be loyal to the values of the organisation,
- Be flexible and willing to change when required by management,
- Be respectful and ethical.

The concept of resilience comes into play here. One definition of resilience is that it reflects an individuals' capacity to cope when immersed in ongoing, stressful contexts (Karatsoreos & McEwen, 2013), and it is this understanding of resilience that supports the neoliberal discourse of individual responsibility. Citizens living in a neoliberal context are positioned as needing to continually adapt to the challenges presented by the world around them. Citizens who do not demonstrate resilience are perceived to be failures. In my figured world this is evident in the willingness of 'academics to buy into the competition required for academic success' (Bottrell & Keating, 2019, p. 161). Thus 'self-management is complicit in the normalisation of overwork as recognisable ways of being academics' (p. 161).

In order to support followers to develop these ideal characteristics and demonstrate resilience, management will offer a range of training opportunities. In my figured world, if a staff member finds him or herself overworked, the solution is to offer a course on time management. If a staff member complains of being bullied, management will offer him/her a course on the code of conduct. If there are complaints about the toxicity of the workplace, staff are referred to a stress management course. If the increasing number of sick leave days being taken, and/or increased referrals to the staff counselling service are identified, management offer a course on managing change. In this figured world, the message from management is that one is never doing enough (Mayo, 2019) and that any problem always lies with the worker, not with management or the system.

Workers are generally so busy managing their day-to-day reality, their capacity to reach beyond their immediate reality to collaborate, to develop a collective position and act from that position, is massively undermined (Arfken, 2018). The 'erstwhile idea of collective responsibility in finding solutions to macro-social problems is destabilized and seduced by the consumption of self-care and wellness products under neoliberalism' (Datta & Chakraborty, 2018, p. 22). Instead, increases in workload, busyness and a focus on making the most for oneself increase competition and decrease collegiality (Hil, 2012). This increase in competition is experienced as a blight on the lives of staff (Mayo, 2019), impacting health and wellbeing. In her report, Liz Morrish (2019) identified increases, in some cases over 300 per cent, in referrals to welfare services for academic staff in the UK.

In the most recent Voice survey at UNE (Voice Project, 2019), only 49 per cent indicated they felt emotionally well at work and 47 per cent identified they could keep their work stress to an acceptable level.

Employees who are happy at work are more productive. Characteristics of the employment context that support employee happiness include (Robert Half, 2017): a match between organisation and employee values, employee empowerment, feeling appreciated, fairness, positive workplace relationships and undertaking interesting and meaningful work. In my figured world whilst many academics are passionate about their work, there is an increasing disjunction between espoused values of management and the experiences of those doing the core work of the organisation. There is an increasing perception that fairness is a dream; exemplified by the inequity between conditions and pay of managers and the workforce, and the perception that the rules are different for management than they are for staff. Management claim increasing power in decision-making so that staff no longer feel empowered, and communications from management that continually cast aspersions on staff (for example, VC Communiqués that call staff morality into question for taking protected industrial action) all contribute to staff unhappiness. In my figured world, the role of followership is one characterized by unhappiness, and an increasing sense of hopelessness given the only strategies to manage this feeling are to either fully engage with neoliberal managerialism and turn oneself into a good neoliberal citizen, or resign.

Work harder

University employees are currently experiencing a level of work intensification that I have never before seen in the sector. Overwork is common and expected (Rea, 2018) and required performance outcomes set targets that are unrealistic to expect within a normal working week. In one study, 62 per cent of research academics reported they felt exploited as their interest (and passion) in their work led to expectations of incredibly high workloads (Shift Learning, 2020). The Wellcome report (Shift Learning, 2020) calls this presenteeism, where nearly a third of researchers reported working over 50 hours a week, feeling pressured to do so. In my figured world and others similar to mine, the targets set for promotion, discussed above, mean that only those who work many more hours than those for which they are paid, are successful. As a consequence for most, work intrudes into private time and private life (Taberner, 2018). The most recent NTEU survey (National Tertiary Education Union, 2017) identified that most academic staff in Australia worked at least 50.7 hours a week (the normal working week for academics should be 37.5 hours) and that professional staff worked 40.7 hours a week (the normal working week for professional staff should be 35 hours a week). Using 2015 figures, this means that academic staff nationally are donating around $1.4 billion a year worth of labour to their employers, and professional staff are donating around $290 million a year worth of labour. Asian academics are reportedly more likely to work at weekends and late into the evenings, based on the results of the Barnett, Mewburn, and Schroter (2019) study that analysed what time of day articles were submitted to the BMJ, however the study demonstrated a consistent culture of overwork internationally. Under neoliberalism, such levels of work intensification are not only expected, they are required given that the ideal neoliberal employee is one who is expected to work constantly, to never rest (Davies & Petersen, 2005).

The consequences of work intensification are evident in increasing levels of stress and ill health (Mitchell, 2019). Watts (2017) reports that whilst around 19 per cent of the general Australian population were identified as at risk for mental health problems, for academics the prevalence rose to nearly 50 per cent. In reality, he claims, the 'tertiary-education system would come to a rapid halt if all those who were entitled to it, decided to take stress leave' (p. 251). The situation is not much better in the UK. In a ground breaking report Morrish (2019) demonstrated a significant increase in referrals to welfare and/or counselling services for UK university staff. Increases of 123 per cent were identified at the University of Bath between 2013 and 2016; 316 per cent at the University of Warwick between 2009 and 2015; and 158 per cent at the University of Leeds between 2010 and 2015. Probably one of the largest increases was observed at the University of Kent where referrals to occupational health services increased by 424 per cent between 2009 and 2015. Women appeared to be more at risk than men, making up 70 per cent of the counselling referrals and 60 per cent of the occupational health referrals. Of the occupational health referrals, 65 per cent were from the ranks of professional staff. This latter is not surprising given that the majority of professional staff appointed at lower levels are women.

The risks for poor mental health outcomes doubles when work stress intrudes into family life (Beattie, 2019). The values associated with neoliberalism (materialism in particular) are linked to reduced happiness in general, with a weak focus on relationships and caring, and poorer wellbeing, even when materialistic goals are achieved. Inequality, another key element of neoliberalism, is also linked to reduced wellbeing and unhappiness (Randle, Eckersley, & Miller, 2017).

Mental health is now recognised as a key factor in workplace safety (Safe Work Australia, 2019) and employers are now expected to take 'reasonable steps to gain an understanding of the psychosocial hazards and risks associated with the operations of the business or undertaking' (p. 8). High job demands are identified in the Safe Work Australia standards as one of the key factors contributing to psychological health hazards. However, my personal experience suggests that despite this recent requirement, management are not able to effectively manage mental health hazards in the workplace because the ideologies that drive them position such hazards as desirable. Work intensification, and the audit culture that drives the measurement and standardisation of work, are important elements in the figured world view of management that contribute towards effective staff supervision and control. Reducing these hazards requires a shift in world view but this is unlikely to happen. As Richards (2019, p. 95) claims there is 'no conspiracy to change this result. It explains why the people in power do nothing about it. They like it. It serves their interests.'

Summary

Whilst there is a growing literature addressing followership as a focus of study in its own right (rather than as an adjunct to leadership) much of that literature focuses on followership in an ideal context where followers and leaders work together for the benefit of an organisation. In my figured world, the role of followership is defined under neoliberal managerialism as one of powerlessness, where compliance and unthinking obedience is expected, and rewarded. Followers are only valued if they comply with management demands, so that success for the organisation is defined as doing what management want. In contrast, followers who think for themselves are positioned as a danger to the organisation (P. Adams, 2019).

This positioning challenges the identities of staff, given most come into higher education with a professional identity in place based on their studies and employment history. In many cases, this professional identity brings with it experiences of professional autonomy and respect that are undermined in the figured world of my university. Successful followership in my figured world involves accepting a lack of autonomy and respect, and yet being expected to be 'nice' whilst professionalism is challenged, disrespected and ignored.

At the same time, the figured world identifies resistance to this identity destruction as inappropriate, and often dangerous. I am expected to accept graciously my positioning as incompetent, the dismissal of my years of experience, in order to follow the instructions of line managers junior to me, with less experience in either the professional or managerial spheres. I am expected to attempt to improve myself (despite being told by more than one manager that I will never be able to do so, presumably because I am labelled a trouble-maker). Despite drowning in over-work, I am expected to demonstrate my willingness to belong by taking on additional tasks, including attending professional development courses (often run by those with less experience in the specific topic than myself) which take a significant chunk of time out of my working week, making it even more difficult to meet my deadlines. Failure to take on this additional load is perceived as my unwillingness to belong, my unwillingness to be a 'good' employee, a 'good' neoliberal citizen.

Happiness in the workplace requires a congruence of values between management and workers. If I am to experience happiness in my figured world of work, I need to challenge the bullshit language that uses words to frame values that sound wonderful in the abstract, but mean something quite different when enacted by management. My follower-ship role requires me to fight for the well-being of the organisation which I contend is being destroyed by neoliberal managerialism. As Elizabeth Warren once said (<https://www.brainyquote.com/quotes/elizabeth_warren_690849?src=t_fight>): 'What I've learned is that real change is very, very hard. But I've also learned that change is possible – if you fight for it.'

CHAPTER 7

Coping with, resisting and changing bullshit

Gusts of laughter echoed down the corridor as I headed down (late) for morning tea. In our building, many of us make a point of collecting in the tea room for morning tea where we share our frustrations, seek the advice of others, and generally spend a little time de-stressing. On this occasion, many were rolling their eyes at the installation of a suggestion box which enabled us to post anonymous ideas of how to improve our school's culture. Proposed suggestions got wilder and wilder as we fed off each previous idea and built the level to one of pure insanity but great hilarity. Everyone was laughing and a couple of others, who don't normally come to morning tea, left their offices and joined us as the laughter was so infectious. Given a recent call for ideas for new courses, someone suggested we develop a new leadership course with units such as 'Developing the most obscure form', 'Bullying 101', and 'Ivory Tower Status Symbols'. Some weeks later, at a school meeting, a manager reprimanded, in public, whoever posted this suggestion in the box, and in doing so, read out the entire suggestion to the school audience. Our harmless joke suddenly became the subject of a whole school reprimand, but one which received many surreptitious giggles as it was being read out. Not long after, the suggestion box in our building mysteriously disappeared. Our collective morning teas continue. We have developed a draft of a board game (the worst move is not being sent to jail, directly to jail without passing go, but being sent to management), and we have a large jigsaw on the go most of the time on which everyone works together. We occasionally have our own informal end-of-day functions where we gather for a small drink before heading home. We celebrate Wombat Day together every year (22 October) with a huge morning tea (why wombats? Why not!), recognise birthdays and achievements (both personal and professional), and we sometimes have a sing-along. We may have little power to change the neoliberal managerial bullshit that rains down upon us every day but together we are able to laugh at some of the more ridiculous examples, and collectively discuss how to manage some of them. There are constant rumours that our building is going to be closed and we will all be moved into the main building.

So far in this book I have shared my experiences of the negative impacts neoliberal managerialism has had on my figured world. I believe that in order to begin to change the ideologies that shape my figured world, I have to understand what they are, and how they operate, seducing people into accepting them and living by their dictates. This exploration has led to this chapter where I reflect on my own experiences of both coping and resisting, and where I look to the literature to help me shape my thinking about how to prompt change. This task is not an easy one. It is clear that neoliberalism, and its enactment in organisations through managerialism, is ubiquitous in our world, and that those living within this framework are strongly influenced by the way these ideologies position them as individuals, and the social world around them. Some even appear to take a TINA approach (there is no alternative) to neoliberalism (Fine & Saad-Filho, 2017). Certainly, the way we behave in our figured worlds is based on our perceptions of what is important in that world (Volker, 2019) and our ability to reflect on our own experiences is influenced by our perceptions of what matters (Stephens, 2003). Thus, my work through this book has served to challenge me to think beyond the kinds of values and behaviours that are expected in my figured world. I begin to shape the values, behaviours and outcomes I think ought to be prioritized in a different kind of figured world to the one in which I currently occupy. I do not believe in a TINA approach to neoliberalism, rather I want to explore other options.

The literature is clear that there is a difference between simply coping, managing to survive in a figured world, to actively resisting what is perceived as not acceptable. Both coping and resisting are based on a recognition that what is happening within a figured world is not acceptable. However, in order to change the figured world, we need to move beyond both coping and resisting and begin to develop an alternative narrative; one that supports the values and practices we believe are better for us, for our students, and for the society in which we operate. In my figured world colleagues move between coping and resisting multiple times a day. Certainly, we all recognise that we cannot resist absolutely everything and that it is important to identify where one's energy can best be targeted. Coping and resisting do not exist as a mutually exclusive dichotomy. Rather, staff are continually acting and reacting to the figured world of which they are a part in different ways depending on each unique combination of circumstance, context and available resources. Building an alternative narrative, however, requires an additional step beyond coping and resisting, and, I think, a form of leadership that is truly democratic in order for the alternative narrative to build organically.

Coping with bullshit

In a figured world that positions workers as incompetent, untrustworthy and in need of micromanagement to perform effectively, it is difficult to maintain a sense of self-efficacy or self-worth. R. Martin (2015) suggests that one of the key skills workers need to do this is emotional intelligence. In this context, emotional intelligence is more than the ability to recognise and regulate emotions in ourselves and others. Rather, I argue, it includes a high level of self-awareness that enables each of us to maintain a core belief in ourselves that is impervious to attack from others. Bottrell and Keating (2019) position this as sustainability of purpose. I imagine this as something like a seed encased inside a hard shell; the hard shell can take a battering, but the seed inside remains undamaged. Emotional intelligence in my figured world also involves the ability to recognise the emotional states of others. This is the ability to recognise that the criticism from a manager does not necessarily imply incompetence on my part, but rather is an expression of the insecurity of the person attempting to put me down, or perhaps their desire to demonstrate their belonging in the figured world of management. It also involves informed decision-making. I may have just been treated like an incompetent idiot, but I have to choose how to respond. An emotional response (getting upset, feeling angry and hurt) is likely to lead to an emotional action (firing off an email complaining that I should not be treated this way). In my experience, this then receives bullshit platitudes in response (for example, I am sure you understand that it is important that we follow policy, and keep the needs of students at the front of our minds) and these only serve to annoy me further. I can choose to ignore the treatment but I find this often festers and I tend to brood about the unfairness of it all (and dream about brilliant repartees I might have made had I thought of them in time). Sometimes I can talk myself out of this pit; I can share it with colleagues and laugh about it, and I can even store it in the file of examples I have kept for this book; a strategy that helps me sleep at night. Sometimes I can respond by being excruciatingly polite; in reality a form of passive aggressiveness where I enclose some kind of subtle dig in a mass of polite bullshit. For example, at one point I sought approval for some additional casual hours (casual because chronic under-staffing meant there were no ongoing staff available to do the work) to amend a unit that was not compliant with our accreditation documentation nor the university's official unit database. The procedure I had always used in the past was to put a case to the relevant person in management explaining the problem and justifying the additional expense. Once that expenditure was approved, I would then submit the contract request form which identified the person who would do the work, the hours and the pay rate. In this case, I did the initial request. I was then told before my request could be considered I had to submit the form which requested the contract for the person the team had in mind to do the work along with the paper making the case for the funding request. This involved additional work that would not be necessary if the request for additional funding was refused as it had sometimes been in the past. However, I did so immediately with a cover email thanking the person concerned for their response, thanking them for informing me of the new process as I was previously unaware of it (with an emphasis on the 'new'). Here I am not claiming that passive aggressiveness is a sign of emotional intelligence: rather the contrary. It is, however, a coping strategy that enabled me to get what I needed from a system that changed the goalposts without any notification, then positioned me as incompetent in not meeting these new (previously unidentified) goalposts.

At other times I have found myself in a situation where I have decided rather than change my practice, to simply engage in what Connell (2019a) calls fake accountability and Bottrell and Keating (2019) subversive compliance. I remember many years ago having to match the learning outcomes of all the units in the range of degrees I was co-ordinating with the appropriate level in the then new Australian Qualifications Framework (AQF). At the time we were all supplied with some key words to use in our learning outcomes for each level: the aim was to demonstrate that students progressed from simple discussion (at first year) through analysis and synthesis to critique (in the final year units) of course content as they progressed through the degree. At the time, my team and I spent weeks amending units to ensure that the appropriate levels of expectation were addressed in each unit. This involved not changing the content itself (as this was subject to accreditation requirements) but the way we expected students to engage in the material and share their understanding in their assessment work. Some years later, the AQF was amended again and levels within some of the courses I was co-ordinating changed. Again, we were provided with a grab-bag of words we could use in our learning outcomes for each level. This time around I dutifully changed the words in my learning outcomes to match the required levels but made absolutely no changes in the course materials to match the change in words used in the learning outcomes to describe student capabilities. Along with Graeber (2019, p. 45) I felt that 'not only does [the] box-ticking exercise do nothing toward accomplishing its ostensible purpose, it actually undermines it, since it diverts time and resources away from the purpose itself.' Thus, the way to best cope with the requirement to engage in this box ticking exercise was to do the minimal amount of work necessary to demonstrate surface compliance, and spend my time more positively by engaging with students as they worked their way through my units.

Whilst not genuinely engaging in each and every box-ticking exercise might be considered somewhat dishonest, it has 'become a necessary skill for university workers' (Connell, 2019a, p. 132). Across many organisations it is becoming clear that workers are increasingly pretending to engage; in Spicer's (2018) words, engaging in simulation. Taberner (2018) calls this covert resistance. For some this is simply a matter of managing as best they can in the hope that something better will show up (Hil, 2012). For those working outside the top universities (the G8 in Australia), there is a risk that something better is less likely to come along (Taberner suggests employment outside the G8 tends to result in being perceived as a less desirable academic) so 'they have no alternative, but to stay and endure' (Taberner, 2018, p. 132).

Endurance is easier when workers disengage, employing what Watts (2017) calls preferred ignorance. Workers close their eyes to much of what goes on around them; workplaces become deserted as many close their doors and hide, whilst others work from home and only come in when absolutely necessary. I am constantly amazed when I talk with people who are genuinely unaware of the significant traumas experienced by staff in offices near them and who profess ignorance of major examples of unfair treatment of their colleagues. I remember fighting the inequity of study leave in one faculty when, in order to take study leave (SSP), academics had to fulfil their full annual teaching load in the calendar year in which they took SSP. In other areas of the university the annual teaching load was pro-rated based on the length of SSP granted. In this particular faculty, colleagues, entitled to six months' SSP, were only granted three months as this was the only time possible if they had to teach two trimesters to complete their full annual teaching load. On top of that reduction, was imposed a requirement that annual leave also had to be a component of the time away, so the actual SSP time was reduced to two and a half months. I tried hard to get colleagues across this faculty to engage in collective action around this inequity but failed to engage anyone other than those directly affected. Some years later, one of the people I had tried to engage came to me with a complaint that s/he had been told s/he had to teach five trimesters in a row in order to teach his/her full annual workload in both of the two years and have SSP in the non-teaching trimester of one of them. His/her SSP length was reduced to two and a half months. All I could do at that point was to say I'm sorry I fought this battle some years ago and lost, and that in fighting the battle I had sought support from all staff but failed to receive it. The tactic of disengagement meant that staff did not understand the inequities happening to their colleagues, and were not willing to try to do so until it directly affected them.

Disengagement may have its benefits as it creates space where workers manage to get their 'real' work done. Spicer (2018) suggests that workers can even create their own bullshit scripts to help 'create a new story for themselves that might allow them to get by' (p. 84). It is my experience that many of my colleagues spend much of the working week engaged in meetings and committees, responding to management requests for information, and form filling. Research work is often squeezed into evenings and weekends. Teaching, particularly in our increasingly online world, also spills over into evenings and weekends. Online tutorials for off campus students are commonly held in the evenings. Marking takes up most weekends. Many of my colleagues position this additional call on their time (many more hours than the 37.5 hours a week for which academics are paid) as their commitment to their students and their desire to do research, rather than as a sign of the unreasonable expectations imposed upon them. Others see this additional work as the route to promotion, and tell themselves that it is necessary to make these kinds of sacrifices if they want to succeed in their careers. Many are so immersed in the neo-liberal managerial figured world, they think it reasonable they should chose to exploit themselves in this way (Spicer, 2018). Coping thus becomes a self-reinforcing narrative that reifies the image of the dedicated academic, of academia as a vocation not just a job. Work in the higher education sector has become a way of life that shapes not just working hours but the entirety of the lives of employees, spilling over to impact on their families and their ability to participate in community life outside of work.

Resisting bullshit

Coping results in the entrenchment of the inequalities, stresses and concerns already discussed in this book, not only in reinforcing managerial privilege, but in shaping worker narratives that contribute towards self-exploitation. For this to change, there needs to be a greater focus on resistance. Resistance requires firstly, that workers identify their self-exploitative narratives and begin to explore other understandings. One alternative narrative is provided in those disciplines associated with a particular profession.

Where a discipline is associated with a particular profession (e.g. engineering, teaching, social work, nursing) academics have a professional identity alongside their higher education identity. They may position themselves as, for example, a botanist academic, an ancient historian academic, a psychologist academic or a teacher academic. This professional identity has its associated practices, ethics and expectations. Our professional identity frames our experiences and shapes how we understand the world around us and our interactions in that world (Yoo, 2019).

Professionalism is associated with professional autonomy; the expectation that within the boundaries of one's expertise, it is appropriate to expect to be able to make professional decisions (Slay & Smith, 2011). Professional identities can thus sometimes provide a buffer which enables their holders to engage in narratives other than those of the figured world of neoliberal managerialism. Professional logic can, in the right contexts, be used to reframe organisational logic (Andersson & Liff, 2018). I have seen colleagues, for example, use professional accreditation requirements to demand more academic staff than management were allowing them, or to maintain a unit with small enrolments that management wanted to delete.

Unfortunately, the figured worlds of most professional bodies are subject to a similar neoliberal managerial ideology, which imposes its own standards and accountability requirements, not all of which necessarily fit within the figured world of higher education. For example, in my own area, one course has to be accredited by two different agencies at state level and another at federal (with a potential fourth body at federal level also indicating future involvement in accreditation). All would be well if the requirements of these bodies were congruent, but unfortunately, they are not. We are left to negotiate a range of contradictory requirements and then try and work out how to fit these into the requirements imposed in our figured world of the university delivering these courses (such as duration of trimesters, placements of practicums within trimesters, rules around when assessments can be due). Sometimes I feel we are trying to complete a 4 dimensional jigsaw with all the pieces of the same colour and with an unknown number missing. Thus, whilst alignment with a profession may create opportunities to explore a different narrative, the reality in my experience, is that the clash of the neoliberal managerial figured worlds of different organisations creates more of a challenge than it offers in opportunities. Resistance to the demands of one figured world through using the demands of another does not challenge the neoliberal managerial ideology underpinning both, but rather reinforces the hegemony of neoliberal managerialism.

Resistance entails identifying behaviours and processes that do not work, that are wrong, and challenging them. Simply accepting bullshit and wrong-doing positions us as part of the problem, not part of the solution (Ball, 2017). However it is important where possible that we do not individualize resistance, as we are stronger together than we are apart (Arfken, 2018). It is important that, having made ourselves aware of the ways in which the figured world acts upon us, we need to identify those elements that are unacceptable and challenge them. We have to be careful in our reflection as we do this because the way we think (our values and beliefs) as well as the language we use, impact on how we interpret our thinking (Locke, 2019). The hegemonic values within a figured world can, and do, shape what we are able to access in our thinking and can render other memories inaccessible to us (Stephens, 2003).

Morrish and Sauntson (2020) suggest that we use metaphors to help us understand the world around us; metaphors that prioritize our values and tell a story in a way that makes us feel comfortable. However, in the same way that Stephens (2003) above noted limits to our thinking imposed by our values, Morrish and Sauntson (2020) note that the metaphors we use can also limit the way we think about our figured world. For example, when we use the metaphor of commerce to position students as customers, we automatically think of student satisfaction as the key indicator of our success in selling our product (education and/or qualifications). The sales metaphor does not enable us to consider evaluating the quality of our teaching and learning in terms of the ways in which it challenges students to think critically, or the way in which it pushes students to perform not only at their best, but perhaps just beyond what they thought they could do. Therefore, our reflective thinking needs to be consciously undertaken, and we need to actively explore ideas and feelings that make

us feel uncomfortable, that challenge us and that offer us different perspectives. We need to be aware of the metaphors we use to understand our
world, and consciously experiment with different metaphors that might
open other avenues in our thinking.

Resistance, if it is not to be futile, must be based on hope that there
is another way, and that finding the other way is possible. In taking about
building hope, Kenway et al. (2015) suggest one strategy is to make decisions about which symbolic acts of defiance are likely to have the most
impact. Industrial action is shaped by a collective discussion about which
acts of defiance are acceptable to the majority and likely to be noticed by
management. Individual acts of defiance are based on individual judgements about what matters most. For example, many colleagues chose to
work at home on a frequent and regular basis and chose not to notify
management they are doing so. Staff decide if they will attend a school
meeting or not (our Enterprise Agreement indicates we are supposed to
attend at least some of these), and if in making this choice, if a formal
apology will be lodged or not. Whilst the actual teaching period for
Education academics is eight weeks (because of placement requirements)
some academics continue to teach online students over a longer 11- or
12-week period.

I have found it useful at times to use the Public Interest Disclosures Act
1994 (PID Act) to report wrong-doing. I recently attended a community
briefing by the Independent Commission Against Corruption (ICAC)
where the speaker emphasized the importance of establishing patterns of
behaviour. As I understood the speaker to say, ICAC have to triage reports
so can often only investigate the most serious, but they do watch for patterns, and when a pattern of repeated reports is established, that pattern
will trigger an investigation. This to me is an important principle I have
used to guide me as to what I should report. In most cases where I have
chosen to report, the issue of concern has not been major, but along with
Hil (2012), I believe there is value in making a complaint for a purpose. In
these cases, for me, it seems that not identifying an inappropriate behaviour
is tantamount to accepting that behaviour as appropriate. In identifying it,
whilst I do not expect a finding of significant wrong-doing, I am also signalling to those involved that the behaviour is unacceptable. Ultimately, if

the behaviour continues, a pattern of reporting can create the space needed for remediation that a single incident cannot.

This is about holding people accountable for their actions. Tingle (2019) argues that wrong-doing is often not challenged because it is the culmination of a sequence of small events; a 'creeping tide of incremental shocks' (p. 1). It is as if people become punch drunk. They no longer react to major events because they are so tired from resisting all the trivia leading up to the inappropriate behaviour or wrong-doing, they switch off. Thus, there is a perception amongst those in power that 'the public isn't watching, and isn't interested' allowing a 'new cavalier approach to accountability' (p. 5) to flourish. Resistance thus requires workers to be watching, to engage in issues, and to challenge in order to demand accountability.

Resistance is about becoming aware of what happens around me in the figured world, and identifying for myself what I can accept and what I feel is inappropriate, inequitable or simply wrong. Resistance is about pushing back, communicating to others in my figured world (colleagues and management) that I am concerned about these particular issues. Resistance is also about teaching students the skills to not just dream an alternative future but to actively work towards that future with their own versions of radical praxis (Hush & Mason, 2019). In other words, resistance itself does not necessarily create the alternative narratives that may change my figured world in any significant manner. To me, resistance is like nibbling around the edge of a slice of cheddar cheese: if I want brie I have to do something more significant than nibbling around the edge of a piece of cheddar. I have to create a whole new way of making cheese. I have to change the managerial bullshit that transmits neoliberal managerialism into my figured world. I have to aim to reduce the way neoliberal managerialism is enacted within my organisation, and create a different narrative to shape my figured world. As Reid (2019, p. 154) argues:

> Unless the core of the neoliberal educational narrative is changed, the removal of one neoliberal tool will only result in its replacement with a new look but the same intent ... What is needed to unsettle the dominance of neoliberalism in education is a new, more progressive, and futures-focused narrative for education with a strong philosophical core.

Changing bullshit

Ball (2017, pp. 242, 243, 244) reminds us that it is difficult to counter bullshit as in doing so we are:

> not engaged in a fair fight. It takes mere seconds to think up a very specific and com-
> pletely bullshit claim ... Inventing bullshit is easy. Fighting it is hard ... and a war that
> is unwinnable. Fact-checking a bullshit claim takes a lot more time and effort than
> making one does, and even then the fact-check spreads to a much smaller audience,
> and doesn't stop the spread of the original claim.

One of the problems in challenging and changing bullshit is the difficulty disentangling facts from not-quite-true facts and interpretations of facts. Bullshit often takes one position, one interpretation, and emphasizes it at the expense of alternative interpretations. Unpicking bullshit is often a matter of judgement – what is important to one person may not be so to another. In addition, bullshit often makes grandiose claims that are not backed up by reality. For example, in my figured world no one would argue that focusing on students is not important. However, in claiming this statement of values, management simultaneously undercut funding for teaching, removed various forms of student support and increased academic workloads so capacity to focus on quality student learning was reduced. Addressing the bullshit claim then becomes an issue, not of challenging the actual claim, but addressing the gap between the rhetoric (the bullshit) and the reality.

This requires an active attempt to dig deep for the meaning behind the bullshit words, the banal platitudes identified by Taylor (2003). We have to remember that a 'platitude is not an epiphany' (Dignan, 2019, p. 181). When we hear the term 'quality student experience' what exactly does that mean? Does it mean allocating 40 minutes of academic time per online student per trimester (the reality)? Does it mean scheduling online tutorials that the majority of students enrolled in the unit cannot 'attend' virtually, and then expecting them to watch a recording of the session (the reality)? When we hear the term 'digital dominance' does it mean an IT system that is hacked by someone outside the university in order to divert staff pay to different bank accounts (the reality for me)? Does it mean a desktop computer that cannot simultaneously manage word and an Endnote library of more than 100 articles (the reality for a colleague)?

When we hear bullshit it is important to also dig deep to try and uncover in what ways the words are trying to mislead; what are the real purposes the bullshit is trying to obscure (Spicer, 2018); what is the 'diseased reasoning' (Smyth, 2017, p. 7). When we read: 'The University reaffirms that our priority must be the success of our students and the maintenance of the highest quality assurance standards; our actions will be guided by these' (Vice Chancellor's Communiqué, 26 September 2019, available publicly at <https://us3.campaign-archive.com/?u=0b102b47b45c5ad5 bb5ffac2a&id=32206b771c>, pp. 3–4 of downloaded version); we could be excused for thinking that 'the university' (in this context management, not the real definition of the university as per the Act) cares about students. However, such a claim was made in the context of industrial action where union members were fighting for sustainable workloads (important for the delivery of quality teaching and learning) and when management had granted a universal extension that would result in large numbers of incomplete results at the deadline for marks submission. Clearly different interpretations of what is needed to support student success are evident here. Benefit accrues to management if the audience for the message believe the words. Critical thinking is needed to probe and to identify the mismatch between the words and the reality. Lack of this ability is identified by Spicer (2018) as one cause of business failure.

Bullshit also offers a chance for scapegoating (Monbiot, 2017) so in challenging bullshit it is also important to look at who (or what group) is being targeted. Recent industrial action in my figured world was positioned as: 'It is my personal view that the local NTEU are pursuing action in order to protect a workload model which most of us are aware is unequitable and antiquated' (VC Communiqué 26 September 2019, available publicly at <https://us3.campaign-archive.com/?u=0b102b47b45c5ad5bb5ffac 2a&id=32206b771c>, p. 1–2 of downloaded version). Throughout this document, it is not hard to identify the implication that NTEU is wilfully punishing students whilst management are nobly attempting to protect them. Errors of fact in the communiqué were addressed in a document subsequently released by the NTEU (this covered evidence to support claims for 13 errors of fact) but, as identified by Ball (2017), no amount of solid evidence overcomes the emotional impact of post-truth claims. In using post-truth, speakers deliberately abandon reasoned argument (Monbiot, 2017) and position the other as the enemy (Ball, 2017):

> The post-truth approach is the approach of the autocrat ... public discourse is simply a clash of competing narratives: a contest which can then be won by the side willing to make the boldest plays towards emotion and mass appeal – often, history has taught us, through the demonization of minority groups. (Ball, 2017, p. 278)

Smyth (2017) argues it is important that we publicly call bullshit: in not doing so, we are giving it power, allowing it to stand as the truth. When we call bullshit, we can ask for the idea to be repeated in English this time. We can ask for specifics and evidence to support what is being said. Ultimately if we do not receive clarification we can chose to walk away and not engage.

Spicer (2018, p. 168) suggests that workers can challenge bullshit by 'using bullshit as a way of purposefully clogging up an administrative system.' I remember a time when the signatures used on our emails were supposed to be approved by management. A number of us decided it was necessary to change our signatures every week, having a different (inspiring for students of course) message of the week, each and every week. Each week we would send off a notification of our new email signature, then follow up several times a day with anxious emails seeking approval so that the new signature could be used legitimately. Within a few weeks this requirement was dropped and I have heard no more about needing an approval for the material contained in my email signature.

Changing neoliberal managerialism

Changing the way people behave within a figured world requires changing the way they think about that world, and their place in that world: that is, changing values and/or changing the metaphors we use to understand our world. Thinking about this leads me to the work around values framing. Values framing (or emphasis framing) is a process used in political communication where certain elements of an issue are emphasized in order to promote a particular position or possible solution (Kaiser, 2019). Values framing provides a theoretical underpinning for what I called, in the past, spin. The basic proposition here is that behaviour is based on perceptions of reality rather than on reality itself (Volker, 2019). This means people make decisions not simply on the basis of facts presented to them. Rather decisions are influenced by prior beliefs and values, and on the way messages are constructed and communicated. In fact, it is possible to change people's behaviour simply by reframing messages (salience emphasis framing) rather than adding any new information (selection emphasis framing) (Kaiser, 2019). Deliberately constructing a message to trigger particular values that lead to particular desired behaviours is not only possible, it is considered both strategic and desirable. To do this it is important to understand the ways in which particular words and values trigger certain behaviours. For example, if a message contained reference to individualistic values then the audience is much more likely to make a decision based on the impact of the issue on them as individuals. If the message contains references to social responsibilities, values, or consequences the audience is more likely to consider these in their decision-making (Kim, 2019).

There appear to be a range of universal values (such as honesty) that we all hold to some degree, and different groups of these values map onto particular attitudes and behaviours (Chenery, 2017). Some values for example map onto competitiveness and selfishness, whilst others map onto co-operation and altruism. People who hold strong values around creativity, responsibility, loyalty, broadmindedness and unity with nature, for example, are much more likely to behave in ways that are both pro-social and environmentally responsible. In contrast, people whose values prioritize wealth, social power, ambition, success and public image are more likely to act in ways that are anti-social and environmentally damaging. However, people do not always act in accordance with their values. If they believe that others do not share their values they are less likely to act, and if they are in a context where their values are not supported they are also less likely to act. This latter is called values priming and it is important because this effect can be used to shape messages in ways that will prompt action. For example, if we want people to act in a pro-social manner (to give money to a cause, for example) then we are more likely to prompt this behaviour if messages focus on compassionate values than we are on selfish values (such as the economic impact of giving).

However shaping the right message to prompt the desired value and behaviour change is complicated by a process called dis-confirmation bias (Kaiser, 2019). Here dissonance caused by information that is contrary to one's values is likely to prompt a retreat into the comfort of pre-existing values, almost as if it is necessary to strongly defend one's position to maintain belonging. This is particularly relevant in the context of neo-liberal managerialism where the privilege associated with management is likely to be strongly defended (Richards, 2019). In the figured worlds of organisations, change tends to be supported by those who benefit from change, rather than those who feel change is not in their self-interest (Schilling, 2019).

The work around values framing suggests that in challenging bull-shit, it is not just necessary to identify the bullshit, and point out the way in which the language used obscures its meaninglessness, but that it is also necessary to carefully select the language used to mount these challenges. If we want to trigger behaviour change, and the underpinning values changes needed to drive this, then it is important that we target the particular values we want to emphasize. This means that we need to engage in acts of radical imagination (Samier, 2018) to create a new narrative (Hartwich & Becker, 2019); a new figured world in which the values of compassion (Boyd & Grant, 2019), empathy, social justice, honesty, equality, friendship, loyalty responsibility (amongst others; Chenery, 2017), are foregrounded. In doing so we need to avoid individualistic values (Chenery, 2017) such as pleasure, ambition, social recognition, authority, wealth, power and success (amongst others). Looking at this through a different lens, I suggest that the messages we share have to create new metaphors; metaphors that contain the values we want to support. Given 'metaphors evoke concepts and feelings that arise from cognitive schema that are activated by the use of particular metaphorical source domains' (Morrish & Sauntson, 2020, p. 12), it is important that we construct metaphors that create different limits to those imposed on us through neoliberal managerial bullshit.

I remember many years ago being told that in order to convince politicians of the importance of my discipline, early childhood, I had to learn to speak their language. I had to learn to tell an economic story that demonstrated how improving funding for programmes in the early years of life benefitted the state in the long term because of the massive return on investment generated (for example, the work of Heckman & Karapakula, 2019). However, the values framing literature suggests that this is a huge mistake as reference to economic benefits triggers individualistic values that make it more unlikely that recipients of the message will respond with increased funding. Instead, I should have been generating messages that focused on values such as compassion, equity and social justice. Taking this into the higher education context, the metaphor of war is often used in neoliberal managerial bullshit to position the university as always under threat, vulnerable to the incursion of competing universities, and needing to attack first in order to survive. The war metaphor justifies expansion into other towns (we have to establish our presence there before others do; we cannot have the competition located so close to us). It justifies the need for staff to be required to change their work at limited notice (now we have a campus in x town, staff are required to travel there to teach, because we have to keep a high profile to prevent the competition moving in). The war metaphor creates a culture where instability and constant vigilance against threat become the new norm for staff (Morrish & Sauntson, 2020), and the ways in which the metaphor influences how staff (and management) think about their figured world becomes so familiar that it is becomes the only reality.

Thus, it seems to me that in creating the new narrative we need to engage in collaborative discussions around the values and metaphors we want to operationalize in our figured world. Then we have to move from discussion to actually exploring what those values would look like in practice. What would an academic workload model look like that was based on prioritizing our responsibility for student and staff wellbeing? What should our teaching look like if we were underpinned by an acceptance of this responsibility rather than on an individualistic value defining student success as the ingestion and subsequent regurgitation of particular content?

Marx (2019) suggests that once we have identified our values, we need to embed them in our practice through rituals. Here rituals are defined as: 'social interactions in which people are physically co-present, focus on a common object, follow a joint rhythm and develop a common mood ... collective effervescence: an enthusiasm that can only be generated in groups' (p. 316). Successful rituals help us feel positive and create feelings of solidarity. Collegial processes are examples of rituals we desperately need to re-establish in the new narrative of higher education (Connell, 2019a). Collegiality should operate not just within the boundaries of the university, but in the connections between the university and the community. The current provider/customer relationship between the university and the community needs to shift to become one of genuine connection (Kenway et al., 2015). This requires ongoing conversations to build a new narrative and new metaphors about what universities ought to be, and how they should best serve our society (Hil, 2019). Edgar and Edgar (2019) suggest there is an important leadership role here for academics functioning as public intellectuals, providing information and leading debate about key issues in our society, as well as contributing to the debate on what education should be. Underpinning this is, of course, the assumption that collective action is important, and part of that collective is a re-imaging of the role of unions. As one of the few remaining collective voices, unions have an important responsibility in contributing to the debate and supporting the sector in the development of a powerful new narrative.

In her recent book, Connell (2019a) provided examples of other narratives; other ways universities and higher education providers can operate that are different than the neoliberal managerialist-driven ways we experience in Australia. It is not my role to copy these examples here, rather I refer the reader to Connell's masterly discussion. The point I do want to make however, is that the existence of these alternatives demonstrates clearly that another way is possible. We are not living in the land of hopeless dreams. It is possible to deliver higher education differently and it is possible to do so within political contexts that are, themselves, heavily influenced by neoliberalism. Another way is possible, we just have to want it enough to fight for it.

The fight is not just limited to the higher education sector, or even the education sector more broadly. Chomsky (2016) argues we are fighting for democracy. We may believe we are living in a democracy, but in reality democracy is increasingly being 'taken away from us' (Klikauer & Tabassum, 2019, p. 90) so we are now living in a plutocracy (Chomsky, 2013a) where we have less and less say (Cody, 2019). In our reality 'control of government is narrowly concentrated at the peak of the income scale, while the large majority "down below" has been virtually disenfranchised' (Chomsky, 2013a, p. 2). We have responded to our decreasing lack of power by losing trust in democracy; by becoming passive in the faces of the challenges we encounter (Monbiot, 2017).

Universities can become more democratic in reality, and not simply perform democracy as theatre (Monbiot, 2016). We need to fight for the right of the majority to be involved in decision making rather than accepting the right of the minority to make decisions for us (Monbiot, 2017). We need to focus on the principles of 'sharing, democracy, inclusion, empowerment, and attachment' (Oplatka, 2016, p. 10).We can involve more staff in governance (J. Ross, 2019a) and in debate over issues and the resultant decision-making. This is about the importance of belonging, of making decisions at local levels by local people (Monbiot, 2019). We need to reach out and create:

> a community based on bridging networks, not bonding networks. Now a bonding network brings together people from a homogenous group, whereas a bridging network brings together people from different groups. And my belief is that if we create sufficiently rich and vibrant bridging communities, we can thwart the urge for people to burrow into the security of a homogenous bonding community defending themselves against the other. (Monbiot, 2019; 13.01)

We can call on different narratives, such as the narratives associated with decolonization and post-colonial thought, to develop new understandings of democracy (Manathunga & Bottrell, 2019b).

Over 15 years ago Stephens (2003, p. 52) wrote: 'true liberation is not a matter of simply swapping roles – but of challenging the system.' We can hide our heads and get by day by day but that will not help new workers coming into our figured world to have any better experiences than our own. We can engage in targeted acts of resistance which might serve to raise awareness but which generally make little long term impact. We can share our ideas of a new narrative and encourage ongoing conversations about the figured world we would like to create. In a rousing TED talk Monbiot (2019) shared a story:

> 9.10: But something has gone horribly wrong. Disorder afflicts the land.

> 9.16: (Laughter)

> 9.18: Our good nature has been thwarted by several forces, but I think the most powerful of them is the dominant political narrative of our times, which tells us that we should live in extreme individualism and competition with each other. It pushes us to fight each other, to fear and mistrust each other. It atomizes society. It weakens the social bonds that make our lives worth living. And into that vacuum grow these violent, intolerant forces. We are a society of altruists, but we are governed by psychopaths.

> 10.03: (Applause)

> 10.12: But it doesn't have to be like this. It really doesn't, because we have this incredible capacity for togetherness and belonging, and by invoking that capacity, we can recover those amazing components of our humanity: our altruism and cooperation. Where there is atomization, we can build a thriving civic life with a rich participatory culture. Where we find ourselves crushed between market and state, we can build an economics that respects both people and planet. And we can create this economics around that great neglected sphere, the commons.

In this book I have followed Monbiot's advice. I have shared my story and I hope I have shown how this story creates a new way of looking at the figured worlds of universities. Through this story I hope I have begun to shape a path that will help us work together to 'tell the story that lights the path to a better world' (14.52).

Bibliography

Adams, P. (2019). The new culture wars in Australian university workplaces. In C. Manathunga & D. Bottrell (eds), *Resisting neoliberalism in higher education. Prising open the cracks* (Vol. 2, pp. 25–42). Cham: Palgrave Macmillan.

Adams, R. (2017). Bath University vice-chancellor quits after outcry over £468 pay. *The Guardian*, 29 November, three pages downloaded. Retrieved from <https://www.theguardian.com/education/2017/nov/28/bath-university-vice-chancellor-quits-after-outcry-over-468k-pay>.

Alvesson, M., & Spicer, A. (2016). *The Stupidity Paradox: The Power and Pitfalls of Functional Stupidity at Work*. London: Profile Books.

American Association of University Professors. (2014). *On trigger warnings*. Retrieved from Washington, DC: <https://www.aaup.org/report/trigger-warnings>.

Anderson, E. (2019). *Private government: How employers rule our lives (and why we don't talk about it)* (Vol. 44). Princeton, NJ: Princeton University Press.

Anderson, L. (2006). Analytic autoethnography. *Journal of Contemporary Ethnography, 35*, 373–395. doi:10.1177/0891241605280449.

Andersson, T., & Liff, R. (2018). Co-optation as a response to competing institutional logics: Professionals and managers in healthcare. *Journal of Professions and Organization, 5*(2), 71–87. doi:10.1093/jpo/joy001.

Anissimov, M. (2013). Principles of reactionary thought. In WordPress (ed.), *More right. Questioning Modernity* (Vol. 2019). <https://archive.is/Tysuy#selection-19.0-23.21>: WordPress.

Anonmyous (2011). Latham savages 'wooden, childless' Gillard. *ABC News*, Monday, 4 April, two pages downloaded. Retrieved from <https://www.abc.net.au/news/2011-04-04/latham-savages-wooden-childless-gillard/2630710>.

Apple, M. W. (2017). What is Present and Absent in Critical Analyses of Neoliberalism in Education. *Peabody Journal of Education, 92*(1), 148–153. doi:10.1080/0161956X.2016.1265344

Arfken, M. (2018). From resisting neoliberalism to neoliberalizing resistance. *Theory & Psychology, 28*(5), 684–693. doi:10.1177/0959354318800393

Askins, K., & Blazek, M. (2017). Feeling our way: academia, emotions and a politics of care. *Social & Cultural Geography, 18*(8), 1086–1105. doi:10.1080/14649365.2016.1240224

Australian Association of University Professors (2019). *What should a university be in 2030?* Retrieved from Sydney: University of Sydney:

Australian Council of Social Services, & University of New South Wales. (2018). *Inequality in Australia 2018*. Sydney: Australian Council of Social Services and University of New South Wales,.

Azevedo, F., & Jost, J. (2019). Neoliberal Ideology and the Justification of Inequality in Capitalist Societies: Why Social and Economic Dimensions of Ideology Are Intertwined. *Journal of Social Issues, 75*(1), 49–88. doi:10.1111/josi.12310

Ball, J. (2017). *Post-Truth: How Bullshit Conquered the World*. London: Biteback Publishing.

Bamberger, A., Morris, P., & Yemini, M. (2019). Neoliberalism, internationalisation and higher education: connections, contradictions and alternatives. *Discourse: studies in the cultural politics of education, 40*(2), 203–216. doi:10.1080/01596306.2019.1569879

Banerjee, P. (2003). Imagining Organizational Transformation through Linguistic Suggestion. *Journal of Human Values, 9*(1), 3–18. doi:10.1177/097168580300900102

Barad, K. (2007). *Meeting the Universe Halfway: Quantum Physics and the Entanglement of Matter and Meaning*. Durham, NC: Duke University Press.

Barcan, R. (2019). Weighing up futures: experiences of giving up an academic career. In C. Manathunga & D. Bottrell (eds), *Resisting neoliberalism in higher education. Prising open the cracks* (Vol. 2, pp. 43–64). Cham: Palgrave Macmillan.

Barnett, A., Mewburn, I., & Schroter, S. (2019). Working 9 to 5, not the way to make an academic living: observational analysis of manuscript and peer review submissions over time. *BMJ, 367*, l6460. doi:10.1136/bmj.l6460

Baronce, E. (2015). *From Passivity to Toxicity. Susceptible followers in a conducive environment.* (Master of Business). Linnaeus University, Växjö, Sweden. Retrieved from <http://www.diva-portal.org/smash/record.jsf?pid=diva2%3A839156&dswid=-1495>.

Bastardoz, N., & Van Vugt, M. (2019). The nature of followership: Evolutionary analysis and review. *The Leadership Quarterly, 30*(1), 81–95. doi: <https://doi.org/10.1016/j.leaqua.2018.09.004>.

Beattie, P. (2019). The Road to Psychopathology: Neoliberalism and the Human Mind. *Journal of Social Issues, 75*(1), 89–112. doi:10.1111/josi.12304

Beattie, P., Bettache, K., & Ching Yee Chong, K. (2019). Who is the neoliberal? exploring neoliberal beliefs across East and West. *Journal of Social Issues, 75*(1), 1–29. doi:10.1111/josi.12309

Bell, D., Canham, H., Dutta, U., & Fernández, J. S. (2019). Retrospective Autoethnographies: A Call for Decolonial Imaginings for the New University. *Qualitative Inquiry, 0*(0), 1077800419857743. doi:10.1177/1077800419857743

Bessant, J. (2015). 'Smoking Guns': reflections on truth and politics in the university. In M. Thornton (ed.), *Through a glass darkly: the social sciences look at the neoliberal university* (pp. 229–255). Acton, ACT: ANU Press.

Bettache, K., & Chiu, C. Y. (2019). The Invisible Hand is an Ideology: Toward a Social Psychology of Neoliberalism. *Journal of Social Issues, 75*(1), 8–19. doi:10.1111/josi.12308

Bhat, A. (2017). Language: the crucial instrument of social control. *Jadavpur Journal of Languages and Linguistics, 1*(1), 35–41. Retrieved from <http://jjll.jdvu. ac.in/journal/index.php/JJLL/article/view/4/17>.

Birch, K., & Springer, S. (2019). Peak neoliberalism? Revisiting and rethinking the concept of neoliberalism. *Ephemera. Theory and politics in organisation, 19*(3), 467–485.

Blackmore, J. (2015). Disciplining academic women: gender restructuring and the labour of research in entrepreneurial universities. In M. Thornton (ed.), *Through a glass darkly: the social sciences look at the neoliberal university* (2 edn, pp. 179–194). Acton, ACT: ANU Press.

Blackmore, J. (2019a). Feminism and neo/liberalism: contesting education's possibilities. *Discourse: studies in the cultural politics of education, 40*(2), 176–190. doi:10.1080/01596306.2019.1569877

Blackmore, J. (2019b). Leadership in higher education. A critical feminist perspective on global restructuring. In S. Wright & C. Shore (eds), *Death of the public university? Uncertain futures for higher education in the knowledge economy* (pp. 90–113). New York: Berghahn.

Blackwood, K., Bentley, T. A., & Catley, B. E. (2018). A victim's search for resolution: Conceptualising workplace bullying and its intervention as a process. *Journal of Health, Safety & Environment, 34*(1), 7–31. Retrieved from <https:// www.researchgate.net/profile/Kate_Blackwood/publication/334151608_A_ victim%27s_search_for_resolution_Conceptualising_workplace_bullying_ and_its_intervention_as_a_process/links/5d1a7701299bf1547c8f75c1/A-victims-search-for-resolution-Conceptualising-workplace-bullying-and-its-intervention-as-a-process.pdf>.

Bottrell, D., & Keating, M. (2019). Academic Wellbeing Under Rampant Managerialism: From Neoliberal to Critical Resilience. In D. Bottrell & C. Manathunga (eds), *Resisting Neoliberalism in Higher Education Volume I: Seeing Through the Cracks* (pp. 157–178). Cham: Springer International Publishing.

Bourassa, G. N. (2019). Postschool imaginaries: Educational life after neoliberalism. *Policy Futures in Education, 0*(0), 1478210318765544. doi:10.1177/1478210318765544

Boyd, B., & Grant, A. (2019). Unveiling opportunities for hope. *Australian Universities' Review, 61*(1), 71–75.

Bozalek, V., & Zembylas, M. (2017). Diffraction or reflection? Sketching the contours of two methodologies in educational research. *International Journal of Qualitative Studies in Education, 30*(2), 111–127. doi:10.1080/09518398.2016.1201166

Braun, S., Kark, R., & Wisse, B. (2019a). Editorial: Fifty shades of grey: Exploring the dark sides of leadership and followership. In S. Braun, R. Kark, & B. Wisse (eds), *Fifty shades of grey: Exploring the dark sides of leadership and followership* (pp. 1–7). Lausanne, Switzerland: Frontiers Media.

Braun, S., Kark, R., & Wisse, B. (eds) (2019b). *Fifty shades of grey: exploring the dark sides of leadership and followership*. Lausanne, Switzerland: Frontiers Media.

Brennan, M., & Zipin, L. (2019). Seeking an institution-decentring politics to regain purpose for Australian university futures. In C. Manathunga & D. Bottrell (eds), *Resisting neoliberalism in higher education. Prising open the cracks* (Vol. 2, pp. 271–292). Cham: Palgrave Macmillan.

Campbell, C. (2018). An interview with Tim Ingold: educational-freedom, the craft of writing, and the university. In *Philosophasters* (Vol. 2019).

Carlen, A. (2018). *is the term neoliberalsim useful?* (BA (Hons) Politics). University of London, Retrieved from <https://www.academia.edu/37605311/Is_the_term_neoliberalism_useful>.

Carroll, T., Clifton, J., & Jarvis, D. S. L. (2019). Power, leverage and marketization: the diffusion of neoliberalism from North to South and back again. *Globalizations, 16*(6), 771–777. doi:10.1080/14747731.2018.1560180

Carroll, T., & Jarvis, D. S. L. (2015). The New Politics of Development: Citizens, Civil Society, and the Evolution of Neoliberal Development Policy. *Globalizations, 12*(3), 281–304. doi:10.1080/14747731.2015.1016301

Ceisel, C., & Salvo, J. (2018). Autoethnographical responses to the political. *Qualitative Inquiry, 24*(5), 307–308.

Chang, H. (2008). *Autoethnography as method*. Walnut Creek, CA: Left Coast Press.

Chang, H. (2013). Individual and collaborative autoethnography as a method: A social scientist's perspective. In S. Holman Jones, T. Adams, & C. Ellis (eds), *Handbook of autoethnography* (pp. 107–122). Walnut Creek, CA: Left Coast Press.

Chenery, M. (2017). A matter of values. *Habitat Australia, 45*(2), 10–13. Retrieved from <https://search.informit.com.au/documentSummary;dn=302294083728499;res=IELAPA>.

Chomsky, N. (2013a). The US behaves nothing like a democracy. Transcript of a speech delivered in Bonn, Germany at DW Global Media Forum. *Salon,*

Saturday, 17 August, 35 pages downloaded. Retrieved from <http://www.salon. com/2013/08/17/chomsky_the_u_s_behaves_nothing_like_a_democracy/>.

Chomsky, N. (2013b). Will Capitalism Destroy Civilization? *TruthOut Op-Ed*, 7 (12 March), four pages downloaded. Retrieved from <http://cpadelhi.org/ opinion/Opinion_12_March_2013_Noam.docx>.

Chomsky, N. (2016). *Who rules the world?* New York: Hamish Hamilton (Penguin Books).

Christensen, L. T., Kärreman, D., & Rasche, A. (2019). Bullshit and Organization Studies. *Organization Studies*, *0*(0), 0170840618820072. doi:10.1177/0170840618820072.

Cleland, J., & Durning, S. J. (2019). Education and service: how theories can help in understanding tensions. *Medical Education*, *53*(1), 42–55. doi:10.1111/ medu.13738

Cody, M. (2019). Neoliberalism, Authoritarianism, and the Crisis of Democracy (Theoretical Perspective). *paper downloaded from Academia*, 1–54. Retrieved from <https://www.academia.edu/32017172/Neoliberalism_ Authoritarianism_and_the_Crisis_of_Democracy.docx?auto=download>.

Connell, R. (2007). *Southern theory. the global dynamics of knowledge in social science*. Crows Nest, NSW: Allen & Unwin.

Connell, R. (2019a). *The good university. What universities actually do and why its time for radical change*. Melbourne, Victoria: Monash University Publishing.

Connell, R. (2019b). Preface. In C. Manathunga & D. Bottrell (eds), *Resisting neoliberalism in higher education. Prising open the cracks* (Vol. 2, pp. v–vii). Cham: Palgrave Macmillan.

Contandriopoulos, D. (2019). About academic bullshit in nursing. *Nursing Inquiry*, *26*(1), e12277. doi:10.1111/nin.12277

Cooper, M., Gulen, H., & Rau, P. R. (2016). *Performance for Pay? The Relation Between CEO Incentive Compensation and Future Stock Price Performance*. Retrieved from Available at SSRN: <https://ssrn.com/abstract=1572085> or <http://dx.doi.org/10.2139/ssrn.1572085>.

Coyne, I., Farley, S., Axtell, C., Sprigg, C. A., Best, L., & Kwok, O. (2017). Understanding the relationship between experiencing workplace cyberbullying, employee mental strain and job satisfaction: a dysempowerment approach. *International Journal of Human Resource Management*, *28*(7), 945–972. Retrieved from <https://dspace.lboro.ac.uk/dspace-jspui/bit-stream/2134/20808/3/Coynecyberbullyingrevisionthreenamed.pdf>.

Da'as, R. a., & Zibenberg, A. (2019). Conflict, control and culture: implications for implicit followership and leadership theories. *Educational Review*, 1–15. doi:10 .1080/00131911.2019.1601614.

Datta, A., & Chakraborty, I. (2018). Are You Neoliberal Fit? The Politics of Consumption under Neoliberalism. In O. Kravets, P. Maclaran, S. Miles, & A. Venkatesh (eds), *The SAGE Handbook of Consumer Culture* (pp. 453–477). London: Sage.

Davies, B. (2005). The (Im)possibility of intellectual work in neoliberal times. *Discourse: studies in the cultural politics of education, 26*(1–14). doi:10.1080/01596300500039310

Davies, B., & Petersen, E. (2005). Neo-liberal discourse in the Academy: The forestalling of (collective) resistance. *Learning and Teaching: the international journal of higher education in the social sciences, 2*(2), 77–98. Retrieved from <https://www.researchgate.net/publication/240748452_Neo-liberal_discourse_in_the_Academy_The_forestalling_of_collective_resistance>.

Davis, E. (2017). *Post truth. Why we have reached peak bullshit and what we can do about it.* London: Little, Brown.

Deckard, S., & Shapiro, S. (2020). World-culture and the neoliberal world-system: an introduction. In S. Deckard & S. Shapiro (eds), *World literature, neoliberalism, and the culture of discontent* (pp. 1–48). Cham: Palgrave Macmillan.

Deleuze, G. (1995). *Negotiations, 1972–1990.* New York: Columbia University Press.

Deleuze, G., & Guattari, F. (1987). *A Thousand Plateaus: Capitalism and Schizophrenia* (trans. B. Massumi). Minneapolis: University of Minnesota Press.

Denzin, N. (1997). *Interpretive ethnography: Ethnographic practices for the 21st century.* Thousand Oaks, CA: Sage.

Denzin, N. (2017). Critical Qualitative Inquiry. *Qualitative Inquiry, 23*(1), 8–16. doi:doi:10.1177/1077800416681864

Dignan, A. (2019). *Brave new work.* London: Penguin Business.

Dumitrescu, I. (2019). Ten rules for succeeding in academia through upward toxicity. *Times Higher Education*, 21 November, three pages downloaded. Retrieved from <https://www.timeshighereducation.com/opinion/ten-rules-succeeding-academia-through-upward-toxicity?utm_source=THE+Website+Users&utm_campaign=13aeffb0ad-EMAIL_CAMPAIGN_2019_11_20_01_00_COPY_01&utm_medium=email&utm_term=0_daa7e51487-13aeffb0ad-62034893>.

Eagleton-Pierce, M. (2019). Neoliberalism. In T. Shaw, L. Mahrenbach, C. Murphy, R. Modi, & X. Yi Chong (eds), *The Palgrave Handbook of Contemporary International Political Economy* (pp. 119–134). London: Palgrave.

Edgar, D., & Edgar, P. (2019). Universities as Failed Critics. In J. Menadue (ed.), *Pearls and Irritations* (Vol. 2019). <https://johnmenadue.com/don-and-patricia-edgar-universities-as-failed-critics/>.

Education and Policy Team (2016). *The Emergence of the Gig Economy. Thought Leader Paper*. Retrieved from Sydney: <https://cdn.aigroup.com.au/Reports/2016/Gig_Economy_August_2016.pdf>.

Ellis, C. (2004). *The ethnographic I: A methodological novel about autoethnography*. Walnut Creek, CA: Rowman Altamira.

Ellis, C. (2007). Telling secrets, revealing lives: Relational ethics in research with intimate others. *Qualitative Inquiry, 13*, 3–29. doi:10.1177/1077800406294947.

Ertas, N., & McKnight, A. N. (2019). Clarifying and reframing the neoliberal critique of educational policy using policy process theories. *Discourse: studies in the cultural politics of education, 40*(2), 234–247. doi:10.1080/01596306.2019.1569881.

Feely, M. (2019). Assemblage analysis: Ran experimental new-materialist method for analysing narrative data. *Qualitative Research*, 1–20. doi:10.1177/1468794119830641.

Feijó, F. R., Gräf, D. D., Pearce, N., & Fassa, A. G. (2019). Risk Factors for Workplace Bullying: A Systematic Review. *International Journal of Environmental Research and Public Health, 19*, 1945–1969. doi:10.3390/ijerph16111945.

Fine, B., & Saad-Filho, A. (2017). Thirteen Things You Need to Know About Neoliberalism. *Critical Sociology, 43*(4–5), 685–706. doi:10.1177/0896920516655387.

Fitza, M. A. (2017). How much do CEOs really matter? Reaffirming that the CEO effect is mostly due to chance. *Strategic Management Journal, 38*(3), 802–811. doi:doi:10.1002/smj.2597.

Foroughi, H., Gabriel, Y., & Fotaki, M. (2019). Leadership in a post-truth era: A new narrative disorder? *Leadership, 0*(0), 1742715019835369. doi:10.1177/1742715019835369.

Fox, N., & Alldred, P. (2017). *Sociology and the new materialism: theory, resarch, action*. Los Angeles, CA: Sage.

Fox, N., & Alldred, P. (2018). Mixed methods, materialism and the micropolitics of the research-assemblage. *International Journal of Social Research Methodology, 21*(2), 191–204. doi:10.1080/13645579.2017.1350015.

Fraher, A. L. (2016). A toxic triangle of destructive leadership at Bristol Royal Infirmary: A study of organizational Munchausen syndrome by proxy. *Leadership, 12*(1), 34–52. doi:10.1177/1742715014544392

Frankfurt, H. (2005). *On bullshit*. Princeton, NJ: Princeton University Press.

Fraser, n. (2013). How feminism became capitalism's handmaiden – and how to reclaim it. *The Guardian*, 14 October, four pages downloaded. Retrieved from <https://www.theguardian.com/commentisfree/2013/oct/14/feminism-capitalist-handmaiden-neoliberal>.

Freire, P. (1973). *Pedagogy of the oppressed*. New York: Seabury.

French, R. (2019). *Report of the Independent Review of Freedom of Speech in Australian Higher Education Providers*. Canberra ACT.

Fuller, N. (2019). Time comes to move on. *Armidale Express Extra*, 3 July, 3.

Furedi, F. (2017). *What's happened to the university? A sociological exploration of its infantilisation*. Abingdon, Oxon: Routledge.

Gann, J. (2018). 6 women on how they've been treated at work after having kids. *The Cut*, June 13, six pages downloaded. Retrieved from <https://www.thecut.com/2018/06/6-women-pregnancy-discrimination-motherhood-workplace.html>.

Gaztambide-Fernández, R. (2011). Bullshit as resistance: justifying unearned privilege among students at an elite boarding school. *International Journal of Qualitative Studies in Education*, *24*(5), 581–586. doi:10.1080/09518398.2011.600272.

Giroux, H. (2015). *Dangerous thinking in the age of the new authoritarianism*. Boulder, CO: Paradigm Publishers.

Gjorgjioska, M. A., & Tomicic, A. (2019). The Crisis in Social Psychology Under Neoliberalism: Reflections from Social Representations Theory. *Journal of Social Issues*, *75*(1), 169–188. doi:10.1111/josi.12315.

Graeber, D. (2015). *The Utopia of Rules. On technology, Stupidity, and the secret joys of bureaucracy*. Brooklyn, NY: Melville House.

Graeber, D. (2019). *Bullshit jobs. The rise of pointless work and what we can do about it*. London: Penguin Random House.

Graeber, D., & Cerutti, A. (2018). *Bullshit jobs*. New York, NY: Simon & Schuster.

Gray, E. M., & Nicholas, L. (2019). 'You're actually the problem': manifestations of populist masculinist anxieties in Australian higher education. *British Journal of Sociology of Education*, *40*(2), 269–286. doi:10.1080/01425692.2018.1522242.

Gschwandtner, A., & McManus, R. (2018). *University vice chancellor pay, performance and (asymmetric) benchmarking, School of Economics Discussion Papers, No. 1807*. Retrieved from Canterbury: <http://hdl.handle.net/10419/189918>.

Hartwich, L., & Becker, J. C. (2019). Exposure to Neoliberalism Increases Resentment of the Elite via Feelings of Anomie and Negative Psychological Reactions. *Journal of Social Issues*, *75*(1), 113–133. doi:10.1111/josi.12311.

Havergal, C. (2019). Australian performance funding puts emphasis on job success. *Times Higher Education*, 2 October, three pages downloaded. Retrieved from <https://www.timeshighereducation.com/news/australian-performance-funding-puts-emphasis-job-success?utm_source=THE+Website+Users&utm_campaign=307a49b8a1-EMAIL_CAMPAIGN_2019_10_02_02_20_COPY_01&utm_medium=email&utm_term=0_daa7e51487-307a49b8a1-62034893>.

Hayes, D. (2019). Vacuous value statements miss the point of higher education, *Times Higher Education*, May 9, three pages downloaded. Retrieved from <https://www.timeshighereducation.com/opinion/vacuous-value-statements-miss-point-higher-education>.

Heckman, J., & Karapakula, G. (2019). *Intergenerational and intragenerational externalities of the Perry Preschool Project*. Retrieved from Cambridge, MA: <https://www.nber.org/papers/w25889.pdf>.

Hil, R. (2012). *Whacademia. An insider's account of the troubled university*. Sydney: NewSouth Publishing.

Hil, R. (2019). Whose future? *Australian Universities' Review, 61*(1), 55–58.

Hill, D. (2004). Books, banks and bullets: controlling our minds – the global project of imperialistic and militaristic neo-liberalism and its effects on education policy. *Policy Futures in Education, 2*(3 & 4), 504–522. doi:10.2304/pfie.2004.2.3.6

Holland, D., Lachicotte, W., Skinner, D., & Cain, C. (1998). *Identity and Agency in Cultural Worlds*. Cambridge, MA: Camridge University Press.

Holman Jones, S. (2016). Living Bodies of Thought:The 'Critical' in Critical Autoethnography. *Qualitative Inquiry, 22*(4), 228–237. doi:10.1177/1077800415622509.

Humle, D. M., & Pedersen, A. R. (2015). Fragmented work stories: Developing an antenarrative approach by discontinuity, tensions and editing. *Management Learning, 46*(5), 582–597. doi:10.1177/1350507614553547.

Hush, A., & Mason, A. (2019). Education as the practice of freedom, from past to future: student movements and the corporate university. *Journal of Philosophy in Schools, 6*, 84–115. doi:10.21913/JPS.v6i1.1569.

Hymas, C. (2018). Vice chancellor salary study demolishes their claims that pay rises are based on performance. *The Telegraph*, 6 June, four pages downloaded. Retrieved from <https://www.telegraph.co.uk/news/2018/06/06/vice-chancellor-salary-study-demolishes-claims-pay-rises-based/?WT.mc_id=tmg_share_em>.

Jagger, J. (2015). The New Materialism and Sexual Difference. *Signs, 40*(2 (Winter)), 321–342. Retrieved from <https://www.jstor.org/stable/10.1086/678190>.

Jakubik, M. (2011). *Becoming to Know: Essays on Extended Epistemology of Knowledge Creation*. (PhD). Hanken School of Economics, Helsinki. Retrieved from <https://helda.helsinki.fi/bitstream/handle/10227/811/223-978-952-232-114-5.pdf?sequence=1>.

Jayasuriya, K. (2015). Transforming the public university: market citizenship and higher education regulatlry projects. In M. Thornton (ed.), *Through a glass darkly: the social sciences look at the neoliberal university* (pp. 89–102). Acton, ACT: ANU Press.

Jenkins, F. (2015). Genderd hierarchies of knowledge and the prestige factor: how philosophy survives market rationality. In M. Thornton (ed.), *Through a glass darkly: the social sciences look at the neoliberal university* (pp. 49–62). Acton, ACT: ANU Press.

Jin, M., McDonald III, B., Park, J., & Trevor Yu, K. (2019). Making public service motivation count for increasing organizational fit: The role of followership behavior and leader support as a causal mechanism. *International Review of Administrative Sciences, 85*(1), 98–115. doi:10.1177/0020852316684008.

Johnes, J., & Virmani, S. (2019). Chief executive pay in UK higher education: the role of university performance. *Annals of Operations Research.* doi:10.1007/s10479-019-03275-2.

Joint Task Force on Teaching Assessment and Evaluation. (2019). *Joint Task Force on Teaching Assessment and Evaluation Recommendations.* Retrieved from Ames, IA: <http://www.facsen.iastate.edu/sites/default/files/uploads/Senate%20Presentations/Teaching%20Task%20Force%20report%20FINAL.pdf>.

Jones, A., & Hoskins, T. K. (2016). A mark on paper: the matter of Indigenous-Settler history. In C. Taylor & C. Hughes (eds), *Posthuman research practices in education* (pp. 75–92). Houndmills, Basingstoke: Palgrave Macmillan.

Juego, B. (2018). Authoritarian Neoliberalism: Its Ideological Antecedents and Policy Manifestations from Carl Schmitt's Political Economy of Governance. *Administrative Culture, 19*(105–136). Retrieved from <https://jyx.jyu.fi/handle/123456789/60133>.

Kaiser, J. (2019). Disentangling the Effects of Thematic Information and Emphasis Frames and the Suppression of Issue-Specific Argument Effects through Value-Resonant Framing. *Political Communication,* 1–19. doi:10.1080/10584609.2019.1658662.

Kangas, A., & Salmenniemi, S. (2016). Decolonizing knowledge: neoliberalism beyond the three worlds. *Distinktion: Journal of Social Theory, 17*(2), 210–227. doi:10.1080/1600910X.2016.1184174.

Karatsoreos, I. N., & McEwen, B. S. (2013). Annual Research Review: The neurobiology and physiology of resilience and adaptation across the life course. *Journal of Child Psychology and Psychiatry, 54*(4), 337–347. doi:10.1111/jcpp.12054.

Keashly, L. (2019). Workplace Bullying, Mobbing and Harassment in Academe: Faculty Experience. In P. D'Cruz, E. Noronha, L. Keashly, & S. Tye-Williams (eds), *Special topics and particular occupations, professions and sectors* (pp. 1–77). Singapore: Springer Singapore.

Keaton, S. A., & Bodie, G. D. (2011). Explaining Social Constructivism. *Communication Teacher, 25*(4), 192–196. doi:10.1080/17404622.2011.601725.

Kelley, R. (1988). In praise of followers. *Harvard Business Review, 66*(6), 142–148.

Kelley, R. (2008). Rethinking followership. In R. E. Riggio, I. Chaleff, & J. Lipman-Blumen (eds), *The Art of Followership: How Great Followers Create Great Leaders and Organizations* (pp. 5–16). Hoboken, NJ: John Wiley & Sons.

Kenway, J., Boden, R., & Fahey, J. (2015). Seeing the necessary 'resources of hope' in the neoliberal university. In M. Thornton (ed.), *Throuh a glass darkly: The social sciences look at the neoliberal university* (pp. 259–281). Canberra: National UNiversity Press.

Kernis, M. H. (2003). TARGET ARTICLE: Toward a Conceptualization of Optimal Self-Esteem. *Psychological Inquiry, 14*(1), 1–26. doi:10.1207/S15327965PLI1401_01.

Khadem, N. (2019a). Blowing the whistle on the Australian Taxation Office could land this man in jail. *ABC News*, 6 March, five pages downloaded. Retrieved from <https://www.abc.net.au/news/2019-03-06/ato-whistleblower-faces-161-years-prison-possibility/10872350>.

Khadem, N. (2019b). CEO bonuses soar as Qantas boss Alan Joyce tops list of highest-paid executives. *ABC News*, 17 September, four pages downloaded. Retrieved from <https://www.abc.net.au/news/2019-09-17/ceo-bonuses-soar-as-qantas-boss-alan-joyce-tops-list/11518356>.

Khalifa, K. (2010). Social Constructivism and the Aims of Science. *Social Epistemology 24*(1), 45–61. doi:10.1080/02691721003632818.

Kim, K. (2019). The Hostile Media Phenomenon: Testing the Effect of News Framing on Perceptions of Media Bias. *Communication Research Reports, 36*(1), 35–44. doi:10.1080/08824096.2018.1555659.

Kinman, G., & Wray, S. (2020). Wellbeing in academic employees– a benchmarking approach In R. Burke & S. Pignata (eds), *Handbook of Research on Stress and Well-being in the Public Sector* (pp. 25 pages downloaded). Cheltenham, Glos: Edward Elgar Publishing.

Kirkby, D., & Reiger, K. (2015). Design for learning? A case study of the hidden costs of curriculum and organisational change. In M. Thornton (ed.), *Through a glass darkly: the social sciences look at the neoliberal university* (pp. 211–227). Acton, ACT: ANU Press.

Klikauer, T. (2013). *Managerialism: a critique of an ideology*. Houndsmills, Basingstoke: Palgrave Macmillan.

Klikauer, T., & Tabassum, R. (2019). Managing bullshit [Book Review]. *Australian Universities' Review, 61*(1), 86–92.

Kock, N., Mayfield, M., Mayfield, J., Sexton, S., & De La Garza, L. M. (2019). Empathetic Leadership: How Leader Emotional Support and Understanding Influences Follower Performance. *Journal of Leadership & Organizational Studies, 26*(2), 217–236.

Koro-Ljungberg, M., MacLure, M., & Ulmer, J. (2018). D...a...t...a..., Data++, Data, and Some Problematics. In N. Denzin & Y. Lincoln (eds), *The SAGE handbook of qualitative research* (5 edn, pp. 462–483). Thousand Oaks, CA: Sage Publications.

Lakes, R. D., & Carter, P. A. (2011). Neoliberalism and Education: An Introduction. *Educational Studies*, *47*(2), 107–110. doi:10.1080/00131946.2011.556387

Langford, S. (2019). Poor Baby Barnaby Joyce says he's 'struggling' on a $211,000 salary. *Junkee*, 29 July, three pages downloaded. Retrieved from <https://junkee.com/barnaby-joyce-struggle-newstart/215880>.

Lather, P. (2019). Updata: Post-Neoliberalism. *Qualitative Inquiry*, *o*(0), 1077800419878749. doi:10.1177/1077800419878749.

Ledesma, M. C., & Calderón, D. (2015). Critical Race Theory in Education: A Review of Past Literature and a Look to the Future. *Qualitative Inquiry*, *21*(3), 206–222. doi:10.1177/1077800414557825.

Lincoln, Y., & Guba, E. (1985). *Naturalistic Inquiry*. Thousand Oaks, CA: Sage.

Linstead, S., Maréchal, G., & Griffin, R. W. (2014). Theorizing and Researching the Dark Side of Organization. *Organization Studies*, *35*(2), 165–188. doi:10.1177/0170840613515402

Lipton, B. (2015). A new 'ERA' of women and leadership. the gendered impact of quality assurance in Australian Higher Education. *Australian Universities' Review*, *57*(2), 60–70.

Lloro-Bidart, T. (2017). A feminist posthumanist political ecology of education for theorizing human-animal relations/relationships. *Environmental Education Research*, *23*(1), 111–130. doi:10.1080/13504622.2015.1135419

Locke, W. (2019). Teaching excellence is not something to aspire to. *Times Higher Education*, 3 June, three pages downloaded. Retrieved from <https://www.timeshighereducation.com/opinion/teaching-excellence-not-something-aspire>.

Loh, J. (2013). Inquiry into Issues of Trustworthiness and Quality in Narrative Studies: A Perspective. *The Qualitative Report*, *18*(33), 1–15. Retrieved from <http://nsuworks.nova.edu/tqr/vol18/iss33/1>.

Lyons, K., & Hill, R. (2018). Million-dollar vice-chancellor salaries highlight what's wrong with our universities. *The Conversation*, 5 February, six pages downloaded. Retrieved from <http://www.abc.net.au/news/2018-02-05/vc-salaries-are-a-symptom-of-whats-wrong-with-our-universities/9396322>.

McKoy, Y. (2013). The queen bee syndrome: A violent super bee. *Journal of Nursing Care Quality*, *2*(3), 200. doi:10.4172/2167-1168.S1.004.

McNally, M. (2018). Academic Freedom. *NTEU Advocate*, *25*(2), 36–37.

Malakyan, P. (2019). Authentic self: Personal identity conceptualizations for leaders and followers (an interdisciplinary study), *Journal of Organizational*

Psychology, *19*(1), 35–59. Retrieved from <http://search.proquest.com.ezproxy. une.edu.au/docview/2211266001?accountid=17227>.

Manathunga, C., & Bottrell, D. (2019a). Prising open the cracks in neoliberal universities. In C. Manathunga & D. Bottrell (eds), *Resisting neoliberalism in higher education. Prising open the cracks* (Vol. 2, pp. 1–22). Cham: Palgrave Macmillan.

Manathunga, C., & Bottrell, D. (2019b). Prising open the cracks through polyvalent lines of inquiry. In C. Manathunga & D. Bottrell (eds), *Resisting neoliberalism in higher education. Prising open the cracks* (Vol. 2, pp. 293–319). Cham: Palgrave Macmillan.

Mannell, J., & Davis, K. (2019). O18 Breaking the gold standard: qualitative methods for trials of complex health interventions. *BMJ Open*, *9*(Suppl 1), A7–A7. doi:10.1136/bmjopen-2019-QHRN.18.

Marshall, R., & Lee, L.-E. (2016). *Are CEOs paid for performance? Evaluating the effectiveness of equity incentives*. Retrieved from MSCI.com: <https://www.msci. com/documents/10199/91a7f92b-d4ba-4d29-ae5f-8022f9bb944d>.

Martin, K. (2018). 'Humpty Dumpty': teaching strategy or postcolonial method – what do we know about power, voice and identity within early chidlhood education in the twenty-first century? In M. Fleer & B. Van Oers (eds), *International Handbook of early childhood education* (pp. 77–90): Springer Netherlands.

Martin, R. (2015). A Review of the Literature of the Followership Since 2008. The Importance of Relationships and Emotional Intelligence. *Sage Open*, *5*(4), 1–9. doi:10.1177/2158244015608421.

Marx, P. (2019). Should we study political behaviour as rituals? Towards a general micro theory of politics in everyday life. *Rationality and Society*, *31*(3), 313–336. doi:10.1177/1043463119853543.3

Matchett, S. (2019). Research burdened by 'bumpf'. *Campus Morning Mail*, 4 July, 1.

Matousek, R., & Tzeremes, N. G. (2016). CEO compensation and bank efficiency: an application of conditional nonparametric frontiers. *European Journal of Operational Research*, *251*(1), 264–273. doi:10.1016/j.ejor.2015.10.035.

Mayo, N. (2019). University staff 'at breaking point' as counselling demand soars. *Times Higher Education*, May 23, four pages downloaded. Retrieved from <https://www.timeshighereducation.com/news/university-staff-breaking-point-counselling-demand-soars?utm_source=THE+Website+Users&utm_campaign=63520eoba1-EMAIL_CAMPAIGN_2019_05_22_01_37_COPY_01&utm_medium=email&utm_term=0_daa7e51487-63520eoba1-62034893>.

Means, A. J., & Slater, G. B. (2019). The dark mirror of capital: on post-neoliberal formations and the future of education. *Discourse: studies in the cultural politics of education*, *40*(2), 162–175. doi:10.1080/01596306.2019.1569876.

Menadue, J. (2019). Here we go again – attacking unions and red tape. In J. Menadue (ed.), *Pearls and Irritations* (Vol. 2019). online: <https://johnmenadue.com/john-menadue-here-we-go-again-attacking-unions-and-red-tape/>.

Milgram, S. (1963). Behavioral study of obedience. *Journal of Abnormal and Social Psychology, 67*(371–378).

Milgram, S. (1965). Some conditions of obedience and disobedience to authority. *Human relations, 18*(1), 57–76. doi:10.1177/001872676501800105.

Milosevic, I., Maric, S., & Loncar, D. (2019). Defeating the Toxic Boss: The Nature of Toxic Leadership and the Role of Followers. *Journal of Leadership & Organizational Studies, 0*(0), 1–21. doi:10.1177/1548051819833374.

Mitchell, C. (2019). 'Continuous improvement' in higher education: Response to 'neoliberalism and new public management in an Australian university: The invisibility of our take-over' by Margaret Sims (2019). *Australian Universities' Review, 61*(2), 57–58.

Monbiot, G. (2016). Neoliberalism – the ideology at the root of all our problems. *The Guardian*, 15 April, eight pages downloaded. Retrieved from <https://www.theguardian.com/books/2016/apr/15/neoliberalism-ideology-problem-george-monbiot>.

Monbiot, G. (2017). *Out of the wreckage. A new politics for an age of crisis.* London: Verso.

Monbiot, G. (2019). The new political story that could change everything. In *TEDSummitt 2019*: <https://www.ted.com/talks/george_monbiot_the_new_political_story_that_could_change_everything/transcript?utm_source=tedcomshare&utm_medium=email&utm_campaign=tedspread#t-9071>.

Montoya, R., & Sarcedo, G. L. (2018). Critical race parenting in the Trump era: a Sisyphean endeavor? A parable. *International Journal of Qualitative Studies in Education, 31*(1), 70–81. doi:10.1080/09518398.2017.1379621.

Morgan, J. (2019). Boss of UK's biggest student housing firm paid £2 million. *Times Higher Education*, 14 August, three pages downloaded. Retrieved from <https://www.timeshighereducation.com/news/boss-uks-biggest-student-housing-firm-paid-2-million-pounds?utm_source=THE+Website+Users&utm_campaign=96ffc87851-EMAIL_CAMPAIGN_2019_08_13_11_25_COPY_01&utm_medium=email&utm_term=0_daa7e51487-96ffc87851-62034893>.

Morris, R. (2015). *Following authentically in the the UK public sector: The importance of visibility, value and voice. Doctoral thesis, Northumbria University.* (PhD). Northumbria University, Newcastle upon Tyne. Retrieved from <http://nrl.northumbria.ac.uk/36009/>.

Morrish, L. (2016). Metaphors we work by. In *Academic irregularities* (Vol. 2019).

Morrish, L. (2017). Why the audit culture made me quit. *Times Higher Education*, 2 March, 10 pages downloaded. Retrieved from <https://www.timeshighereducation.com/features/why-audit-culture-made-me-quit>.

Morrish, L. (2018). Can critical university studies survive the toxic university? In *Academic irregularities* (Vol. 2019).

Morrish, L. (2019). *Pressure Vessels: The epidemic of poor mental health among higher education staff*. Retrieved from Oxford: <https://www.hepi.ac.uk/wp-content/uploads/2019/05/HEPI-Pressure-Vessels-Occasional-Paper-20.pdf>.

Morrish, L., & Sauntson, H. (2020). *Academic irregularities. Language and neoliberalsim in higher education*. New York: Routledge.

Moss, P. (2019). Gilles Deleuze. Thought, movement and (more) experimentation. In P. Moss (ed.), *Alternative narratives in early childhood. An introduction for students and practitioners* (pp. 109–140). Abingdon, Oxon: Routledge.

Murray, D. S. (2019). The precarious new faculty majority: communication and instruction research and contingent labor in higher education. *Communication Education, 68*(2), 235–245. doi:10.1080/03634523.2019.1568512.

National Tertiary Education Union. (2017). *2015 NTEU State of the Uni survey. Report #2 Workloads*. Retrieved from Melbourne, Victoria.

Nawaz Khan, S., Halim Busari, A., & Mariam Abdullah, S. (2019). The Essence of Followership: Review of the Literature and Future Research Directions. In Y. Hayat Mughal & S. Kamal (eds), *Servant Leadership Styles and Strategic Decision Making* (pp. 148–171). Pennsylvania: IGI Global.

Newfield, C. (2018). *The Great Mistake. how we wrecked public universities and how we can fix them*. Baltimore, MD: Johns Hopkins University Press.

O'Keefe, T., & Courtois, A. (2019). 'Not one of the family': Gender and precarious work in the neoliberal university. *Gender, Work & Organization, 26*(4), 463–479. doi:10.1111/gwao.12346

O'Neill, P., & Weller, S. (2013). To what extent has Australia's development trajectory been neoliberalist? *Human Geography, 6*(2), 69–84.

Oplatka, I. (2016). 'Irresponsible Leadership' and Unethical Practices in Schools: A Conceptual Framework of the 'Dark Side' of Educational Leadership. In A. Normore & J. Brooks (eds), *The Dark Side of Leadership: Identifying and Overcoming Unethical Practice in Organizations* (Vol. 26, pp. 1–18). Bingley, UK: Emerald Group Publishing Limited.

Orr, A. J. (2019). Teaching Sociology: The Precariousness of Academic Freedom. *Sociological Perspectives, 62*(1), 5–22. doi:10.1177/0731121418814597

Ortner, S. B. (2019). The ongoing life of patriarchy in neoliberal America. In T. Oren & A. Press (eds), *The Routledge Handbook of Contemporary Feminism* (pp. Chapter 4, no page numbers). Abingdon, Oxon: Routledge.

Orwell, G. (1944; ebook 2016). *Animal Farm*. Adeliade, SA: University of Adelaide Library: ebbos@adelaide.

Padilla, A., Hogan, R., & Kaiser, R. B. (2007). The toxic triangle: Destructive leaders, susceptible followers, and conducive environments. *The Leadership Quarterly*, *18*(3), 176–194. doi: <https://doi.org/10.1016/j.leaqua.2007.03.001>.

Palumbo, A., & Scott, A. (2018). Introduction. In *Remaking market society. A critique of social theory and political economy in neoliberal times* (pp. 1–9). Abingdon, Oxon: Routledge.

Pennington, J. L., & Prater, K. (2016). The veil of professionalism: An autoethnographic critique of white positional identities in the figured worlds of white research performance. *Race Ethnicity and Education*, *19*(5), 901–926. doi:10.1080/13613324.2014.885431.

Percy, A., & Beaumont, R. (2008). The casualisation of teaching and the subject at risk. *Studies in Continuing Education*, *30*(2), 145–157. Retrieved from <http://ro.uow.edu.au/asdpapers/139>.

Pietraszewski, D. (2019). The evolution of leadership: Leadership and followership as a solution to the problem of creating and executing successful coordination and cooperation enterprises. *The Leadership Quarterly, in press. corrected proof.* doi: <https://doi.org/10.1016/j.leaqua.2019.05.006>.

Pilgrim, D. (2017). The Perils of Strong Social Constructionism: The Case of Child Sexual Abuse. *Journal of Critical Realism*, *16*(3), 268–283. doi:10.1080/147674 30.2017.1303928.

Price Waterhouse Coopers, & Australian Higher Education Industrial Association. (2016). *Australian Higher Education workforce of the Future*. Retrieved from <https://www.aheia.edu.au/cms_uploads/docs/aheia-higher-education-workforce-of-the-future-report.pdf>.

Prilipko, E. (2019). Follower Attributes: Perceptions of Leadership and Followership Experts in the United States. *Journal of Leadership, Accountability and Ethics*, *16*(2). doi: <https://doi.org/10.33423/jlae.v16i2.2022>.

Raaper, R. (2019). Assessment policy and 'pockets of freedom' in a neoliberal university: A Foucauldian perspective. In C. Manathunga & D. Bottrell (eds), *Resisting neoliberalism in higher education. Prising open the cracks* (Vol. 2, pp. 155–175). Cham: Palgrave Macmillan.

Radd, S. I., & Grosland, T. J. (2018). Desirablizing whiteness: A discursive practice in social justice leadership that entrenches white supremacy. *Urban education*, 0042085918783824. Retrieved from <https://journals.sagepub.com/doi/pdf/10.1177/0042085918783824?casa_token=JRy1Rq3G-8EAAAAA:s-oHLnYiHSq201Dz2hEKmAGJd63Ga-gjkLdCuRvTC-50TDu26FCxcbiEUI 46NCUAMQgcjE66zFYWUw>.

Randle, M., Eckersley, R., & Miller, L. (2017). Societal and personal concerns, their associations with stress, and the implications for progress and the future. *Futures*. doi: <http://dx.doi.org/10.1016/j.futures.2017.07.004>.

Rea, J. (2018). Breaking the culture of overwork. *NTEU Advocate*, *25*(1), 40–41.

Reid, A. (2019). *Changing australian education. How policy is taking us backwards and what can be done about it*. Crows nest, NSW: Allen & Unwin.

Rhodes, C., & Fleming, P. (2018). CEO pay is more about white male entitlement than value for money. *The Conversation*, 24 July, three pages downloaded. Retrieved from <https://theconversation.com/ceo-pay-is-more-about-white-male-entitlement-than-value-for-money-100245?utm_medium=email&utm_campaign=Latest%20from%20The%20Conversation%20for%20July%20 25%202018%20-%20107229508&utm_content=Latest%20from%20The%20 Conversation%20for%20July%2025%202018%20-%20107229508+CID_c3 aa9c523fea22aaee6c177b9140e19e&utm_source=campaign_monitor&utm_ term=CEO%20pay%20is%20more%20about%20white%20male%20 entitlement%20than%20value%20for%20money>.

Richards, H. (2019). Bullshit Jobs. *Journal of Critical Realism*, *18*(1), 94–97. doi:10.1 080/14767430.2019.1572942.

Robert Half (2017). *It's time we all work happy(TM). The secrets of the happiest companies and employees*. Retrieved from Menlo Park, CA: <https://www. roberthalf.com.au/sites/roberthalf.com.au/files/pdf/noindex/robert-half-australia-its-time-we-all-work-happy-2017.pdf?utm_source=roberthalf&utm_ medium=pressrelease&utm_campaign=rh-all-workhappy2017-ongoing>.

Robertson, L. H., & Hill, D. (2014). Policy and ideologies in schooling and early years education in England:Implications for and impacts on leadership, management and equality. *Management in Education*, *28*(4), 167–174. doi:10.1177/0892020614550468

Rodgers Gibson, M. (2019). Towards a neoliberal education system in Aueensland: preliminary notes on senior secondary schooling reforms. *Policy Futures in Education*, *18*(8), 983–999. doi:10.1177/1478210319833250

Ross, D., Sasso, M., Matteson, C., & Matteson, R. (2020). Narcissistic and Sociopathic Leadership and the World of Higher Education: A Place for Mentoring, Not Mobbing (pages 69-103). In C. Crawford (ed.), *Confronting Academic Mobbing in Higher Education: Personal Accounts and Administrative Action* (pp. 69–103). Hershey, PA: IGI Global.

Ross, J. (2019a). Corporate veterans take over Australian university governance. *Times Higher Education*, 16 May, three pages downloaded. Retrieved from <https:// www.timeshighereducation.com/news/corporate-veterans-take-over-australian-university-governance?utm_source=THE+Website+Users&utm_

campaign=31f42b960b-EMAIL_CAMPAIGN_2019_05_20_07_10&utm_
medium=email&utm_term=0_daa7e51487-31f42b960b-62034893>.

Ross, J. (2019b). Has university governance lost touch with academic reality? *Times Higher Education*, 16 May, 10 pages downloaded. Retrieved from <https://www.timeshighereducation.com/features/has-university-governance-lost-touch-academic-reality>.

Ross, J. (2019c). Hostility to teaching-only universities 'boils down to sentiment'. *Times Higher Education*, 1 July, three pages downloaded.

Ross, J. (2019d). More Australian Vice-Chancellors earning A$1 mission. *Times Higher Education*, 9 September, four pages downloaded. Retrieved from <https://www.timeshighereducation.com/news/more-australian-vice-chancellors-earning-a1-million?utm_source=THE+Website+Users&utm_campaign=f1de9feb90-EMAIL_CAMPAIGN_2019_09_09_08_56&utm_medium=email&utm_term=0_daa7e51487-f1de9feb90-62034893>.

Ross, J. (2019e). Students 'want universities to find jobs for them'. *Times Higher Education*, 27 May, three pages downloaded.

Roth, W.-M. (2009). Auto/ethnography and the question of ethics. *Forum: Qualitative Social Research*, *10*(1), Article 38, 10 pages. doi:10.17169/fqs-10.1.1213.

Rowe, E. (2019). Capitalism without capital: the intangible economy of education reform. *Discourse: studies in the cultural politics of education*, *40*(2), 271–279. doi:10.1080/01596306.2019.1569883.

Rowe, E., Lubienski, C., Skourdoumbis, A., Gerrard, J., & Hursh, D. (2019). Exploring alternatives to the 'neoliberalism' critique: new language for contemporary global reform. *Discourse: studies in the cultural politics of education*, *40*(2), 147–149. doi:10.1080/01596306.2019.1579409.

Rowlands, J., & Rawolle, S. (2013). Neoliberalism is not a theory of everything: a Bourdieuian analysis of *illusio* in educational research. *Critical Studies in Education*, *54*(3), 260-272. doi:10.1080/17508487.2013.830631.

Rudgard, O. (2018). Vice Chancellors can go to meetings which set their own pay at almost all universities. *The Telegraph*, 15 February, three pages downloaded. Retrieved from <https://www.telegraph.co.uk/news/2018/02/15/vice-chancellors-can-go-meetings-set-pay-almost-universities/>.

Ruske, R. (2015). Does Economics Make Politicians Corrupt? Empirical Evidence from the United States Congress. *Kyklos*, *68*(2), 240-254. doi:10.1111/kykl.12082.

Safdar, S., & van de Vijver, F. (2019). Acculturation and its application: a conceltual review and analysis. In K. O'Doherty & D. Hodgetts (eds), *The SAGE Handbook of applied social psychology* (pp. 3–22). London: SAGE Publications Ltd.

Safe Work Australia. (2019). *Work-related psyxhological health and safety. A systematic approach to meeting your duties. National Guidance material.* Canberra, ACT: Safe Work Australia.

Samier, E. A. (2018). Education in a troubled era of disenchantment: the emergence of a new Zeitgeist. *Journal of Educational Administration and History, 50*(1), 41–50. doi:10.1080/00220620.2017.1399865.

Saunders, M. (2006, 2006/03//). The madness and malady of managerialism. *Quadrant, 50*(3), 9–17. Retrieved from <http://link.galegroup.com/apps/doc/A143723603/EAIM?u=dixson&sid=EAIM&xid=b7f5c954>.

Schilling, M. (2019). *Harnessing self interest: effects of framing value orientation on environmental concern and engagement for the wolves.* (Master of Psychology). Maastricht University, Maastricht, Netherlands. Retrieved from <https://www.researchgate.net/profile/Michelle_Schilling/publication/335842439_Harnessing_Self-Interest_for_Environmental_Engagement_Effects_of_Framing_Value_Orientations_on_Environmental_Concern_and_Engagement_for_the_Wolves/links/5d7fdb33a6fdcc66b001a628/Harnessing-Self-Interest-for-Environmental-Engagement-Effects-of-Framing-Value-Orientations-on-Environmental-Concern-and-Engagement-for-the-Wolves.pdf>.

Schwartz, J. (2019). Resisting the norming of the neoliberal academic subject: building resistance across the faculty ranks. In C. Manathunga & D. Bottrell (eds), *Resisting neoliberalism in higher education. Prising open the cracks* (Vol. 2, pp. 65–88). Cham: Palgrave Macmillan.

Shattock, M. (2019). *University governance and academic work: the 'business model' and its impact on innovation and creativity.* London: Centre for Global Education.

Shibata, S. (2019). Gig Work and the Discourse of Autonomy: Fictitious Freedom in Japan's Digital Economy. *New Political Economy*, 1–17. doi:10.1080/1356346 7.2019.1613351.

Shift Learning. (2020). *What researchers think about the culture they work in.* Retrieved from London: <https://wellcome.ac.uk/sites/default/files/what-researchers-think-about-the-culture-they-work-in.pdf>.

Shore, C. (2010). Beyond the multiversity: neoliberalism and the rise of the schizophrenic university. *Social Anthropology, 18*(1), 15–29. doi:10.1111/j.1469-8676.2009.00094.x.

Shore, C., & Wright, S. (2019). Privatizing the public university. Key trends, countertrends and alternatives. In S. Wright & C. Shore (eds), *Death of the public university? Uncertain futures for higher education in the knowledge economy.* (pp. 1–27). New York: Berghahn.

Sims, M. (2018). Achieving the Impossible. *NTEU Advocate, 25*(3), 46–47.

Sims, M. (2019a). 'Bullying is not tolerated here: we have policies and procedures which protect staff.' An auto-ethnography of frustration. *Sociology Insights*, *3*(1), 10 pages. doi:in press version available <http://www.sciaeon.org/sociology-insights/articles-in-press>.

Sims, M. (2019b). Neoliberalism and new public management in an Australian University: the invisibility of our take-over. *Australian Universities' Review*, *61*(1), 22–30. Retrieved from <http://www.aur.org.au/current/pdf>.

Sims, M., & Tiko, L. (2019). Neoliberalism and Post-colonialism in conflict: hybridisation in early childhood in the South Pacific. *New Zealand International Research in Early Childhood Education Journal*, *22*(1), 15–30. Retrieved from <https://www.childforum.com/research/2019-nz-international-early-childhood-education-journal/1686-indigenous-early-childhood-education.html>.

Slay, H. S., & Smith, D. A. (2011). Professional identity construction: Using narrative to understand the negotiation of professional and stigmatized cultural identities. *Human Relations*, *64*(1), 85–107. doi:10.1177/0018726710384290.

Smith, D. G., Rosenstein, J. E., Nikolov, M. C., & Chaney, D. A. (2019). The Power of Language: Gender, Status, and Agency in Performance Evaluations. *Sex Roles*, *80*(3), 159–171. doi:10.1007/s11199-018-0923-7.

Smyth, J. (2017). *The toxic university. Zombie leadership, academic rock stars and neoliberal ideology*. London: Palgrave Macmillan.

Spicer, A. (2018). *Business bullshit*. Abingdon, Oxon: Routledge.

Stahl, R. M. (2019). Economic Liberalism and the State: Dismantling the Myth of Naïve Laissez-Faire. *New Political Economy*, *24*(4), 473–486. doi:10.1080/1356 3467.2018.1458086.

Stahlke Wall, S. (2016). Toward a Moderate Autoethnography. *International Journal of Qualitative Methods*, *15*(1), 1609406916674966. doi:10.1177/1609406916674966

Stanley, D. (2017). Followership. In D. Stanley (ed.), *Clinical Leadership in Nursing and Healthcare. Values into action* (2 edn, pp. 47–58). Chichester: Wiley Blackwekk.

Stephens, J. (2003). The rhetoric of women's leadership: language, memory and imagination. *Journal of Leadership & Organizational Studies*, *9*(3), 45–60.

Suleiman, Y. (2019). Impact of Social Policy on Stability in Capitalism. *Central Asian Review of Economics & Policy*, *1*(1), 33–47. doi:10.15604/carep.2019.01.01.004.

Taberner, A. M. (2018). The marketisation of the English higher education sector and its impact on academic staff and the nature of their work. *International Journal of Organizational Analysis*, *26*(1), 129-152. doi:doi:10.1108/IJOA-07-2017-1198.

Takayama, K., Heimans, S., Amazan, R., & Maniam, V. (2016). Doing southern theory: towards alternative knowledges and knowledge practices in/

for education *Postcolonial directions in education*, 5(1), 1–24. Retrieved from <http://projects.um.edu.mt/pde/index.php/pde1/article/download/72/115#page=7>.

Taylor, P. (2003). Waiting for the Barbarians and the Naked Emperor's Chicken. *Higher Education Review*, 35(2), 5–24.

Thornton, M. (2015). Introduction: The retreat from the critical. In M. Thornton (ed.), *Through a glass darkly: the social sciences look at the neoliberal university* (2 edn, pp. 1–15). Acton, ACT: ANU Press.

Tingle, L. (2019). Politicians keep shifting the goal post as though the public isn't watching. *ABC Online*, Saturday, 26 October, five pages downloaded.

Tuli, F. (2010). The basis of distinction between qualitative and qualitative research in social science: reflection on ontological, epistemological and methodological perspectives. *Ethiopian Journal of Education and Science*, 6(1), 96–108. Retrieved from <https://www.ajol.info/index.php/ejesc/article/viewFile/65384/53078>.

Tyson, L. (2006). *Critical Theory Today: A User-Friendly Guide* (2 edn). New York: Routledge.

University of Aberdeen. (2016). Reclaiming our university. The manifesto. In *Reclaiming our university* (Vol. 2019).

Van Hiel, A., De keersmaecker, J., Onraet, E., Haesevoets, T., Roets, A., & Fontaine, J. R. J. (2019). The relationship between emotional abilities and right-wing and prejudiced attitudes. *Emotion*, 19(5), 917-922. doi:10.1037/emo0000497.

Verger, A., Fontdevila, C., & Parcerisa, L. (2019). Reforming governance through policy instruments: how and to what extent standards, tests and accountability in education spread worldwide. *Discourse: studies in the cultural politics of education*, 40(2), 248–270. doi:10.1080/01596306.2019.1569882.

Verhaeghe, P. (2014). Neoliberalism has brought out the worst in us. *The Guardian*, 29 September, four pages downloaded. Retrieved from <https://www.theguardian.com/commentisfree/2014/sep/29/neoliberalism-economic-system-ethics-personality-psychopathicsthic>.

Voice Project. (2019). *UNE Engagement survey 2019*. Retrieved from Armidale, NSW.

Volker, L. (2019). Looking out to look in: inspiration from social sciences for construction management research. *Construction Management and Economics*, 37(1), 13-23. doi:10.1080/01446193.2018.1473619.

Vygotsky, L. (1962). *Thought and knowledge* (trans. E. V. Hanfmann). Cambridge, MA: MIT Press.

Wadhwa, V. (2016). The best companies in the world are run by enlightened dictators. *Quartz*, 8 June, four pages downloaded. Retrieved from <https://qz.com/701895/the-best-companies-in-the-world-are-run-by-enlightened-dictators/>.

Watts, R. (2017). *Public universities, managerialism and the value of higher education.* London: Palgrave Critical University Studies.

West, D. (2016). The managerial university: a failed experiment? *Demos,* 14 April, nine pages downloaded. Retrieved from <http://demosjournal.com/the-managerial-university-a-failed-experiment/>.

Windle, J. (2019). Neoliberalism, imperialism and conservatism: tangled logics of educational inequality in the global South. *Discourse: studies in the cultural politics of education, 40*(2), 191–202. doi:10.1080/01596306.2019.1569878.

Winkler, I. (2018). Doing Autoethnography: Facing Challenges, Taking Choices, Accepting Responsibilities. *Qualitative Inquiry, 24*(4), 236-247. doi:10.1177/1077800417728956.

Withers, G. (2015). The state of the universities. In M. Thornton (ed.), *Through a glass darkly: the social sciences look at the neoliberal university* (2 edn, pp. 103–120). Acton, ACT: ANU Press.

Wood, A. J., Graham, M., Lehdonvirta, V., & Hjorth, I. (2019). Networked but Commodified: The (Dis)Embeddedness of Digital Labour in the Gig Economy. *Sociology, 0*(0), 0038038519828906. doi:10.1177/0038038519828906.

Woodrow, C., & Guest, D. E. (2017). Leadership and approaches to the management of workplace bullying. *European Journal of Work and Organizational Psychology, 26*(2), 221–233. doi:10.1080/1359432X.2016.1243529.

Wright, C. (2019). *The rise of the right in the United States.* Retrieved from paper downlaoded from <https://www.academia.edu/38706238/The_Rise_of_the_Right_in_the_United_States?email_work_card=view-paper>, 8 April: 23 pages.

Wright, N., & Losekoot, E. (2016). Interpretative research paradigms: Points of difference. In R. McClean (ed.), *Proceedings of the 11th European Conference on Research Methods: ECRM* (pp. 416–422). Reading: Academic Publishing.

Yoo, J. (2019). Creating a positive casual academic identity through change and loss. In C. Manathunga & D. Bottrell (eds), *Resisting neoliberalism in higher education. Prising open the cracks* (pp. 89–107). Cham: Palgrave Macmillan.

Young, K. Z. (2017). Workplace Bullying in Higher Education: The Misunderstood Academicus. *Practicing Anthropology, 39*(2), 14-17. doi:10.17730/0888-4552.39.2.14.

Zheng, Y., Graham, L., Epitropaki, O., & Snape, E. (2019). Service Leadership, Work Engagement, and Service Performance: The Moderating Role of Leader Skills. *Group & Organization Management,* 1059601119851978.

Index